My Sandwich is a Spaceship

My Sandwich is a Spaceship

Creative Thinking for Parents & Young Children

Cyndi Burnett & Michaelene Dawson-Globus

(And Illustrated by Your Family & You!)

ICSC Press
International Center for Studies in Creativity
Buffalo State, State University of New York
Buffalo, NY, U.S.A.

ICSC Press
International Center *for*
Studies *in* Creativity
Buffalo State · The State University of New York

ICSC Press
International Center for Studies in Creativity
SUNY Buffalo State
1300 Elmwood Avenue
Buffalo, NY 14222, USA
icscpress.com

ISBN (print edition): 978-0-9849795-5-4

Library of Congress Control Number: 2015952916

Simultaneously published in multiple formats, both print and electronic. For alternative versions, visit icscpress.com

All trademarks are the property of their respective owners. Web links were accurate at the time of publication, and could, of course, change.

As with all things related to parenting, please use your own best judgment when trying out the ideas and activities in this book. Neither the authors nor the publisher can be held responsible for injury, embarassment, and other misadventures.

To our mothers,
Chris Argona and Mary Ann Dawson,
for showing us every day
what it means to be creative.

Contents

Introduction   **1**

Part One: Setting Meaning and Purpose   **13**

Chapter One: Why Are Creative Thinking Skills Important?   15

Chapter Two: Embracing Your Creativity   25

Chapter Three: The Creative Home   43

Part Two: Digging Deeper   **55**

Skill #1: Curiosity   57

Skill #2: Mindfulness   69

Skill #3: Embrace Challenges   83

Skill #4: Look at it Another Way   101

Skill #5: Produce and Consider Many Alternatives   113

Skill #6: Playfulness   125

Skill #7: Make it Swing! Make it Ring!   141

Skill #8: Visualize It Richly and Colorfully   153

Skill #9: Enjoy and Use Fantasy   163

Skill #10: Be Aware of Emotions   177

Afterword: Extend the Learning   **191**

The End of This Journey: Authors' Reflections   193

Affirmations   196

Acknowledgments   197

About the Authors   201

Contents

Introduction ... 1

Part One: Setting Meaning and Purpose ... 13

Introduction: Why We're All Here, Right Now, Together

This book is about two of our favorite topics: creativity and children. We have written it because we believe it is never too soon to start teaching kids how to use their creativity.

If you have ever spent time watching your children, you might think they are highly creative already. They sing, dance, talk to imaginary friends and invent the most wonderful excuses for why they don't have to go to bed. But creativity is much more than that.

Creativity is the highest form of *thinking.* Creative thinking is a way of seeing the world, a way of solving problems, a way of thriving in an environment that is constantly changing.

This book is about teaching your child the creative skills needed to be successful, no matter what he or she chooses to do in the future. These skills can, and should, last a lifetime, and you can help your child to learn them and use them, starting today.

About This Book

Like parenting, a book is a journey. And together, the readers and authors will explore many paths along the way, much like parents and children.

This book is a creative journey that we will take together. Your authors, Cyndi and Michaelene, will walk you through what we've learned about creativity from (at least) four perspectives: as students and scholars of creativity; as practitioners of creativity and the creative process; as creative human beings; and as creative-minded parents. As a reader, you can try out and try on the ideas and skills we recommend to see how they work for you.

Maybe you don't see the connection between creativity and parenting quite yet. But think about it: as parents—let's face it, it's true—we're making it up as we go along. We are continuously figuring out the solutions to new problems. If that sounds like you at all, it means you are already being a creative parent! Modern, progressive parents (as opposed to old-style, "this is how it's always been done" parents), walk the landscape of parenting by continuously trying things to find out what works, and what doesn't.

Wanting to be a creative parent is the first half of the equation. The other half is wanting to also encourage creativity in your children.

Most of us think our children are creative, at least when they are young. One key question we explore in this book is: *How might you help your child to be even more creative?* Another is: *How might you help your child stay creative for life?*

What does it mean to be creative for life?

This is time that you might ask: *What are you talking about? Isn't creativity just about arts and crafts, and music and acting?*

Allow us to clarify (which, as it happens, is a creativity skill): Creativity is a vast landscape in and of itself, at least as vast and varied as parenting. It can't be summed up in one sentence, but perhaps we can do it justice in two paragraphs:

> *Creativity is a uniquely human phenomenon in which one visualizes a future and conceives a way to make that future a reality. The work of creativity is to produce an outcome that can be defined as creative: a novel and useful result.*

> *As defined in our culture, creativity encompasses cognitive processes and abilities such as the use of language, problem solving, and discovery; and also includes the many forms of creative expression found in the arts.*

Note what's important here: Yes, creativity includes artistic expression, but merely as a subset of the highest-order form of thinking—creative thinking. Creative thinking is not just a nice-to-have skill. It's not even just an important skill. We believe that the ability to think creatively is *the essential life skill* for the 21st Century.

Why do we feel so strongly about this subject? Because at its core, creative thinking is the ability to successfully deal with change. Our children are living and growing in a century that has, and will continue to have, an unprecedented level of change.

Simply put, successfully navigating change is about continuously inventing the future, and learning the skills to get you there.

Now, you may be asking yourself: *Isn't that what schools are supposed to do?* Unfortunately, the answer is no! Well, more correctly, the answer is that ideally it would be great if that's what our teachers were doing. But they're not trained, measured, or rewarded for teaching creative thinking in their classrooms.

We have enormous gratitude and respect for school teachers. As the bumper sticker says, "If you can read this, thank a teacher." The best teachers care about our children deeply, putting every ounce of their abilities into igniting a passion for learning in their students, and they often *do* understand the importance of creative thinking. But they are working within a system that is so focused on traditional measures of performance—that is, what students have memorized, and maybe what they understand—that there is little room for the highest forms of learning: evaluation and creation.[1] The effect of all this—unintentionally, but assuredly—is to squeeze the creativity out of our young ones.

The schools will not preserve and foster our children's creativity. We, as parents and guardians, have to do it, and we have to start when they are young. That's why we wrote this book.

---

[1] Many schools use "Bloom's Taxonomy" to create learning activities. The construct, first published in 1956 and updated in 2001, identified six categories of cognitive processes in learning. They can be thought of as a progression from lower-order to higher-order thinking skills. According to the 2001 revision, they are, from lowest to highest: remember, understand, apply, analyze, evaluate, create. Source: Anderson, L.W., et al. (2001). *A Taxonomy for Learning, Teaching, and Assessing: A revision of Bloom's Taxonomy of Educational Objectives.* New York, NY: Pearson, Allyn & Bacon.

Why should you read this book?

We've explained now why we wrote this book. But why should you read it?

The purpose of this book is to show you how to maximize your child's creative thinking skills as a way of forever changing how they see and approach life, and assuring that they are ready for this rapidly-changing 21st century world.

This book is not a "be the best parent" book, nor will it teach you how to help your child sleep, eat, or socialize with other children. What it *will* do is share with you what we've learned about creative thinking and how it's used in parenting young children. It will provide you with a new language that you can share with your children. It will supply you with a number of activities, tools, and techniques that you can use *right now* to become a more creative family. And it will help you to find *the questions you need to ask* to be a more effective problem solver.

Ultimately, this book will show you a path, using creative thinking, for taking these ideas and turning them into options that work for you.

Children are constantly changing, and it's often difficult to keep up. The minute you find a solution to a challenge that works for your children, they change, and new challenges arise. Each day provides parents with numerous problem-solving opportunities. We evolve as our children evolve. We become more intuitive about our children as time goes on, and can often sense what our children need as we begin to understand who they are as people. Likewise, our children evolve as we evolve. They become more intuitive about *us*, and they learn how to understand us as people, rather than as mere providers of food, clothing, shelter, and security.

You and your child will take this journey of creative discovery together. (And because you're doing it with the help of this book, we're coming along, too.)

What's in this book

My Sandwich is a Spaceship is divided into two parts.

Part One focuses on *you* as the creative parent, and we highly recommend you start there. The goal of Part One is to foster more creative thinking in *your* everyday life.

Part Two focuses on *your child and your family*, providing ten creative thinking skills we believe are important for young children to develop.

Throughout the book, in both Part One and Part Two, are boxes that ask you to participate in the creation of this book. (More about that in a moment.)

You may decide to read the book from start to finish, and then go back and select activities you would like to try. Or you may want to select one skill a week and focus on that particular skill with your family. We designed this book so that each skill not only builds on the next, but complements the other skills.

Here are the ten skills that we cover:

★   Curiosity

★   Mindfulness

★   Embrace Challenges

★   Look at it Another Way

★   Produce and Consider Many Alternatives

★   Playfulness

★   Make it Swing! Make it Ring!

★   Visualize it Richly and Colorfully

★   Enjoy and Use Fantasy

★   Be Aware of Emotions

The first three skills on the list come directly from our experiences in working with young children and parents in the field of creative thinking. The remaining skills were adapted from E. Paul Torrance and H. Tammy Safter's *Making the Creative Leap Beyond*, where the authors described skills related to the creative person.

Each chapter focuses on one creativity skill and contains the following sections:

1. A quote that highlights the essence of the skill.

2. A description of the skill and why it is important for creativity.

3. A story from our experiences that depicts the skill in action.

4. "Cultivate the Language" lists of words and phrases that can boost problem-solving vocabulary.

5. "Set the Tone!" behaviors you can practice to bolster your creativity.

6. "Give It a Go!" activities to dig deep and experiment with the skill.

7. "Keep It Up!" suggestions to continuously develop creative thinking in your family.

We do not want creativity to be an occasional activity for your family, something you might do to get through this one particular car trip or summer vacation. Our overall goal is to have creative thinking become a *mindset* in your home, part of the way in which you and your children *think* and *behave*. We firmly believe that if you begin to nurture these skills in your children at an early age, and if you continue to think about creative thinking skills as your parenting journey continues, then you will be equipped to foster these skills in your children as they enter school and beyond.

Some of the language we ask you to use with your children may seem too "grown up," but we guarantee if you use and teach words such as *mindful, alternative,* and *solving the challenge,* your child will understand, and these words will become part of your child's everyday vocabulary. Here's why it matters: this isn't simply an activity book. We are introducing you to *a way of life.* Our goal is to equip you with the knowledge and skill set for you and your child to be creative, and to continue to grow as creative individuals for the rest of your lives.

The advice we offer is grounded in research, yet it's also practical. We don't expect you to do it all, and we don't expect you to do it perfectly. There is no "perfect." Part of the joy of creativity is realizing that we learn through our failures and our mistakes. Remember: it's a journey, so don't worry. If you are able to follow some of the key principles some of the time, you will be providing a wonderful gift for your children, one that will last throughout their lifetimes. Plus, it's actually a lot of fun! And we'll prove that to you along the way with our stories.

How to use this book

Perhaps the most important thing to understand about this book is that it's *yours.*

My Sandwich is a Spaceship is not meant to be read through and then put away, like most books. It's meant to be a living guide to creativity for you and your family. When we put on the cover "Illustrated by your family and you," we meant it. Throughout this book are places for you and your kids to draw and write, doodle and play.

You might be hesitant to write in the book. We understand; it's not a common thing. Most of us were taught in school that to write in a book was to deface it. We say: embrace it. And do it right away. As soon as you or your child make the first mark in the book, you'll be liberating it from its off-the-press condition. This book *wants* to be marked up. Really, we mean it. Do it for the book's sake.

One other idea: as you read the book, *mark the ideas that you think you'll want to try.* This book is filled with lists of ideas. Some will fit your family better than others. Read with a pencil nearby, and circle those items that resonate with you.

And try to be a little daring, marking some things that you think might make you uncomfortable. Like writing in the book, you'll find that pushing yourself in a new direction gets easier with practice.

Are you ready to get started? On the next page, write your names and draw yourselves. Take ownership of this book and this journey. After all, it's all yours.

SHARE YOUR CREATIVE JOURNEY WITH US!
Take pictures of your drawings and tweet them to @ICSCreativity, with the hashtag #SandwichSpaceship

This book
belongs to:

1

Part One: Setting Meaning and Purpose

Write down all of the reasons you're reading this book.

Chapter One: Why Are Creative Thinking Skills Important?

Do you think your child is creative?

If you have a young child, you probably have witnessed some interesting behavior, such as putting underwear on his head, dipping her orange slices in ketchup, or decorating a pumpkin in a Picasso style. But is that creativity? The answer is yes! It's not world-changing creativity—ketchup and orange slices won't produce a new superfuel that solves the energy crisis (at least, we don't think it will)—but it fits the definition of creativity as the generation of novel and useful ideas. For your child, ketchup and orange slices together make a new combination, and she is probably not afraid to take a risk and see what it tastes like. This kind of curiosity is the fuel of creativity.

If you ask people what creativity is, they are likely to think of eminent, world-changing creativity: great painters or musicians, inventors or innovators. Yet creativity is that and so much more. Yes, producing works of great genius is creativity; so, too, is solving problems in new ways, whether they are large or small. Beyond production, creativity is also about a person: it is a mindset and approach to everything we do. It's about living life in a way that is open, authentic, and curious. Creativity, then, is not only relevant in the arts, but is essential in education, business, science, math, language, health, and, well, everything!

What's useful about underwear on the head? For a child, maybe it's part of imaginative play, which is very useful in cognitive development. Maybe it's part of learning where underwear actually should be worn, which is useful developmentally. Or maybe it's just funny—that's useful, in its own way.

An amazing thing about young children is that they are still discovering what is "right" or "wrong," and they're not afraid to test their ideas and boundaries. They're also not afraid to fail. If you spend some time observing children, you will likely witness their openness to new experiences, their curiosity to discover (that's why they ask so many questions, not simply to annoy us!), and their mastery of trial and error. This is the creative mindset. And while this mindset blossoms in the early years, it often fades once children enter the school system. They learn that there's only one answer to a question, that they shouldn't ask too many questions, and that they should censor their ideas before they are shared ("this won't work because..."). E. Paul Torrance placed the beginning of the decline at the fourth grade, and he had 40 years of studies to confirm it.[2]

But...can someone be too creative?

---

[2] Torrance, E. P. (1967). *Understanding the fourth grade slump in creative thinking*. Washington, DC: U.S. Office of Education. Retrieved from http://files.eric.ed.gov/fulltext/ED018273.pdf

One day, as I (Cyndi) peered through a window, observing my son's preschool class, I saw him happily playing with a box which contained sticker letters. However, he wasn't actually playing with the stickers. Instead, he was using the box as a spaceship, flying it gently throughout the room. I couldn't help but smile at his imaginative play. After a few minutes, the teacher went over to my son, took the box out of his hands, showed him the letters and gave him a piece of paper to stick them on. My smile became a frown. He was quietly playing and using his imagination. Why did this teacher take that away from him?

I don't for a moment believe the teacher intended to squash his imaginative play. Rather, she was simply pushing him toward the appropriate use of the box. And here is the key word: "appropriate." We do need to help our children understand when it is appropriate to use their creativity, and that is through a case-by-case process of discovery. It may be appropriate for your child to try on her shirt fifteen different ways when she is two and you are having a restful day at home. It is not appropriate for her to try on her shirt fifteen different ways when she is five and late for school. In the example above, my son was not disrupting the class, and his behavior was appropriate. If he had been working on an assignment with the rest of the class using the letters, and turned his box into a spaceship, then it would have been inappropriate.

A question, then: How do we allow children to continue developing their creativity within the appropriate context?

First and foremost, they need our parental support and guidance. We set the stage by modeling creative thinking, and by setting a household environment for creativity (see Chapters Two and Three). Second, we need to help them foster and nurture the creative thinking skill sets they were born with. In this book, we will focus on ten essential skills of the creative person. And while there are more than ten skills a productively-creative adult could master, our experience and research tell us that these ten skills are the most important to introduce, encourage, and strengthen creative thinking at an early age.

Why are creative thinking skills important?

In the introduction, we made an argument for the importance of creative thinking as *the* 21st century life skill. It's not a unique argument; you will find many teachers, educational thought leaders and reformers, and even some politicians saying the same thing. But why is it seen as such an important skill, and why now? We would like to offer five reasons.

What does creative thinking look like?
What does it feel like?

1 Creative thinking is required every day for every person

To live is to experience problems. And every time you are faced with a challenge that doesn't have an obvious solution, creativity is required. Small challenges, such as running out of Band-Aids on the day your little one scrapes his leg, and big problems, like finding good child care, all require creativity. Everyone has problems and, therefore, everyone needs to have the skill set to solve these problems in appropriate and meaningful ways. Creative thinking is a means to improve lives and make the world a better place. Creative problem-solving skills can provide you, and your children, with the confidence to work through challenges. Most importantly, when you teach your child about creative thinking and model the same behaviors, you will become a family that works more effectively together. (We will explore this topic in more depth in Chapter Two.)

> Creative thinking is a means to improve lives and make the world a better place. Creative problem-solving skills can provide you, and your children, with the confidence to work through challenges.

2 A creative life can lead to a more joyful life

We are born to create, explore, wonder, think, learn, and grow; to ask questions, make discoveries, and add our own touch to this brilliant and beautiful world. Children remind us of the inherently creative quality of life and the joy that comes with it. Next time you are watching your child engaged in play, pay close attention to how joyful she is. Witness the excitement in her eyes as she asks questions. Think about the smile on his face when he creates a solution to his problem. Observe the laughter when he enters into his imaginative world of play.

The joy of creativity is not just for childhood; it can be a consistent and sustained way of approaching and living life. When we, at any age, are able to embrace our creativity and deliberately develop and nurture our creative skills, the world opens up to us in meaningful and joyful ways.

3 We are in a creativity crisis

Kyung Hee Kim found in a recent study that creativity in children from grades K-6 was clearly and significantly decreasing when compared to previous generations.[3] We could offer several hypotheses on why that is happening: too much time in front of the television, not deliberately teaching creativity in schools, or the need for children

---

3 Kim, K.H. (2011). The creativity crisis: The decrease in creative thinking scores on the Torrance Tests of Creative Thinking. *Creativity Research Journal, 23*(4), 285-295.

to conform to standardized tests. But the best thing we can do as parents is to focus our energies on understanding creativity and deliberately nurturing it in our own homes. This will help to develop a foundation for a creative mindset when our children enter school and move forward through their educational experiences.

The future isn't like it used to be

The 21st century is marked by greater access to information, rapid changes in technology, and increased global connection. Our world is changing at such a high rate that many of our ideas become outdated almost before we have the chance to fully understand them. For this reason, creative thinking is necessary to manage, navigate, and effectively engage in our increasingly complex world. Our children will be inheriting a world that is very different from the world of our youth. Or perhaps we should say, inheriting and *creating*. As parents who recognize the importance of creativity, we can help our children to develop the creative thinking skills needed to embrace, learn about, and thrive in this exciting century that they will be co-creating with their fellow citizens.

Creative thinking will help prepare our children for future career success

Think about what jobs were like thirty years ago, when we were kids. Now, look around at jobs today. With technological developments increasing at an ever faster rate, computers are allowing us to do things we would never have thought we could do. For example, with a few clicks of a button, you can plan your vacation, file your taxes, and pay your bills, all tasks that used to be completed by people in the workforce.

Now, imagine what jobs will be like when our kids enter the workforce. Trend analyzers believe that many jobs that we have now won't exist in the future,[4] and that more than half of our children will work in jobs that *haven't even been invented yet.*[5,6] How do we prepare our children for the future if we don't even know what jobs will exist?

The answer is right here: teach our kids to think creatively and to develop their creative thinking skills, so they'll be prepared *no matter what the future looks like.* Creative thinking is a skill that never loses its standing in the marketplace.

4 CBRE & Genesis. (2014). *Fast forward 2030: The future of work and the workplace.* Richardson, TX: Genesis. http://www.cbre.com/o/international/AssetLibrary/Genesis%20Report_Exec%20Summary_1029.pdf
5 Cornell University ILR School (1999). *Futurework: Trends and challenges for work in the 21st Century.* U.S. Department of Labor. Retrieved from http://digitalcommons.ilr.cornell.edu/cgi/viewcontent.cgi?article=1066&context=key_workplace
6 Davidson, C.N. (2012). *Now you see it: How technology and brain science will transform schools and business for the 21st Century.* New York, NY: Penguin.

List or draw all of the ways you think you're creative.

Chapter Two:
Embracing Your
Creativity

Parenting: There is no instruction manual, but there is creative thinking

Wouldn't it be great if your child came with an instruction manual? If, the moment you first embraced your child, you were handed a detailed parenting guide for raising your beautiful, tiny person? An instructional guide filled with diagrams, pictures and words of wisdom for being a great parent to your unique child?

No one gave you an instruction manual when your child was born. No one told you how to solve the multitude of new and ambiguous challenges that came up daily. The truth is, we create the instruction manual as we go along. Parenting is the ultimate on-the-job training. It requires decision making, problem solving, questioning, and information gathering. We do our best, we experiment, we make mistakes, we learn, we try again, and we grow. And, whether we realize it or not, we do all this by using our creative thinking skills.

Being a parent is wonderful, and it might just be the most difficult job we will ever have. Admit it: there have been moments or even days that the joys of parenting, the sunshine and rainbows, become clouded over by seemingly insurmountable challenges. Those moments when our little angels seem to magically transform into little anarchists. When a missed nap, hungry belly, or testing of boundaries gets us so frustrated that we want to put *ourselves* in a time out. These moments can be difficult to manage, but with creative thinking, they can transform into new opportunities: opportunities to look at things in different ways, to try something new, and to learn more about ourselves and our children.

For example, when my (Cyndi's) son was four years old, he often enjoyed pretending to be a car. He would flap his arms, and spin them around, and make a VROOOOM noise that was loud enough for the neighbors to hear. And while I encourage imagination, he sometimes wanted to be a car at inappropriate times. My worry and concern over my little car became greater when he entered preschool. As I walked through the parking lot, my little car was driving around. I used my creative thinking in all different ways. I tried to get him to be an airplane. An animal. A "big boy." *Anything* to break the car habit. One day, I decided to ask the teacher about his behavior.

"Have you seen James as a car?" I asked, a bit embarrassed.

"Yes!" his teacher happily replied.

I winced. "And is his behavior disruptive?"

"Sometimes it is okay to be a car in my class. And sometimes, I ask him to park his car in the corner, and join us as James. And guess what? It works!"

This simple technique shifted my perspective and helped us to find a solution where he could continue to use imagination and do so at appropriate times.

This is just one example of using deliberate creative thinking to overcome a parenting challenge, and I was grateful to learn this from my son's teacher. If I had received an instruction manual when my son was born, it would have been much easier! But with a little creative thinking from a wise teacher, the same success was achieved.

And while creative thinking can help us to work through challenges that arise, the most beautiful thing about being deliberately creative with parenting is that it nurtures joyful, meaningful, and authentic family relationships. We are working toward developing a family that is compassionate, mindful, open to new possibilities, and engaged with one another. A family that takes the time to enjoy and celebrate the good.

The purpose of this chapter is to help you become a deliberately creative parent, to help you recognize when you are being creative, to embrace your own creativity, and to exercise it with intention.

Do this, please: Before you continue reading this chapter, take a few minutes to consider the following questions. You might find it helpful to use the space provided on the next two pages and write down your answers in depth, rather than just thinking about them.

In what ways are you creative?

When was a specific time you used your creativity to solve a problem?

When was a time you could have used your creativity to solve a problem, but didn't?

Where do you feel the most creative?

Embracing Your Own Creativity: Being a Creative Role Model

It's not only children who grow. Parents do too. As much as we watch to see what our children do with their lives, they are watching us to see what we do with ours. I can't tell my children to reach for the sun. All I can do is reach for it, myself.
— Joyce Maynard

One morning, I (Cyndi) watched my three-year-old daughter playing with her dollhouse. She had a baby doll and a mommy doll. I listened closely to the dialogue she created between the two dolls.

With her sweet baby voice, she said, "I love you. I love you too. Now it is time to go potty! Okay Mommy! Now it is time to go to bed! Okay Mommy!"

Then her voice changed to something a little bit deeper. "I said go to bed."

Then her voice dropped into a register that sounded like a demon's. "I said go to bed!"

Part of me couldn't help but giggle, as this is what happens night after night during our bedroom routine. Everything is peachy until she won't go to bed and I firmly go into my deeper voice. The other part of me realized, through her role-play with her dolls, how much children echo our own behaviors. (But surely I don't sound like a demon. Do I?)

As parents, we are the role models of our families. We also have the great responsibility and privilege of guiding our families as we grow together. Becoming a creative family starts with parents modeling creative thinking behaviors. We know our children are watching us and picking up on our behaviors, attitudes, and actions. We see it when our children use words or phrases that we use, and in the way our children behave on a day-to-day basis.

Therefore, developing and expressing *your own* creativity is one of the most important things you can do to nurture *your child's* creativity. As you grow as a creative person, you also naturally establish the space for your child's creativity to grow and flourish. You make creativity a foundational part of life. You also become an advocate for creativity in environments that may limit your child's creativity. You know it is important, and you protect and nurture it. When we help to nurture the creative power in our children, we are empowering them to overcome the challenges of life, and joyfully live the lives they choose to dream.

Here are six ways to embrace and develop your personal creativity.

> *Developing and expressing your own creativity is one of the most important things you can do to nurture your child's creativity.*

1 Declare your personal creativity

We are going to lead you through a little experiment. We would like you to declare out loud, "I am a creative person." (It's okay if you have to leave the room and be by yourself to do this.)

Now, say it with feeling: "*I am a creative person!*"

How does it make you feel? A little foolish, perhaps, to be talking to yourself. But how does the *message* make you feel? Exhilarated, perhaps, knowing you are releasing your inner creative self to the world? Or worried, maybe, thinking back to the myths associated with creativity—such as how creative people must be artistic or crafty? Is there doubt—doubt that you are truly creative?

The reality is that people who *believe* they are creative are more likely to *be* creative, to exhibit creative characteristics. We could probably debate the chicken-egg of that statement, but let's just take it at its face value: often just announcing (admitting) that you are creative will cause you to think of yourself *as* creative.

Imagine that! Declaring your creativity can cause a shift in your thinking and provide you with the internal freedom you need to *make the statement true.* Well, you don't have to imagine it: you can do it. You can choose to tap into and to develop your creativity. We challenge you to assert it again: "I am a creative person!"

Now that you have declared your creativity, you might want to look back at the box at the beginning of the chapter and see if there are more items you need to add to it!

2 Get back in touch with your inner creative child

Man is most nearly himself when he achieves the seriousness of a child at play. — Heraclitus

Another way to tap into your creativity is to think back to your own childhood. When were you most alive with creative power? Remember the things you were curious about, played with, and imagined.

Chances are that your memories are deeply rooted in creative thinking. Perhaps you remember a time when you were out in nature exploring the world. Perhaps it was a time when you created something that made you feel proud: a story, a fort, a school project, a macaroni art piece, cut-out cookies, or a puppet show. Perhaps it was inventing a game with the neighborhood kids, or creating something fantastic with sidewalk chalk. Remember how much fun that was?

When I (Michaelene) think back to my childhood, I recall being completely enchanted with my mother's jewelry box, or enthralled by the GI Joe world my brother and I created. I remember spending hours playing in the snow, and arguing with my mother, "No, I don't need to come in to warm up," even though the tip of my nose was close to the frostbite zone. It did not matter that I was cold—I was in a place where anything was possible and I was alive with creative power.

Take some time now to reflect on your childhood. Think about the person you were when you were a child. The following list of questions can help you to remember and reconnect to your inner child. Give yourself some time to reflect back on your happy childhood memories.

★ What childhood moments come to mind first?

★ What do you remember playing?

★ What specific games, toys, people, or events brought you joy?

★ Who were your childhood friends? What do you remember doing?

★ What books, movies, and songs were important to you?

★ What did you do outside?

★ What did you do on a rainy day?

★ What did you want to be when you grew up?

★ What spaces and places were special to you?

★ What smells, sounds, and tastes do you remember?

★ What were your favorite foods?

★ What did you collect?

★ What fascinated you?

Take one of the questions from the previous page and write it below. Then, answer the question in any way you like. Get your child to make a drawing of your answer.

Next, describe what you were like as a child. Find a picture of yourself when you were a child and spend a few minutes just looking at your younger self. Observe your face, look into your eyes. Now imagine that you are sitting with your childhood self. What positive things would you say to that younger version of you? What would that child say to you? Imagine that the two of you are playing. What might you be doing? What does that child's laugh sound like?

As you connect to your inner child, look for ways to embrace aspects of that childhood self in your current life.

 ## Give yourself time for creativity

Now that you have spent some time reflecting on your inner creative child, you will need to carve out some time for your adult creativity. Time is a gift we frequently give to others but often neglect to give to ourselves. We know what you are thinking. Time? Who among us with small children also has spare time on our hands to focus on our creative selves? Believe us, it's possible. Here are two ideas:

Take yourself out for a creativity date. Book a specific day and select a creative activity you used to enjoy doing or a new activity you would like to explore. Find a babysitter for a couple of hours, and let yourself go and play! It doesn't need to be every day or even every week; just a few hours a month will make your creativity come alive. Cyndi's creativity dates have included writing in a quiet library, hitting the craft store and making a painting, going to a cooking class, and even taking a tap dance class! Michaelene's creativity dates have included taking a bubble bath, playing a video game, taking a solitary hike in the forest, and making homemade strawberry jam. Think about the things that are difficult to do with your child, and go and do it for yourself. We recommend that you start by keeping a list of fun things you would love to do/try if you had the time. (You can begin right now, in the box below.) Then give yourself the gift of time, and make this time with your creative self a priority.

What are some creative activities you'd like to try?

Become an Adventure Buddy with your child. Instead of observing your child in creative play, engage with him in exploring, wondering, thinking, learning, and discovering. Take your Adventure Buddy on a date: go the local museum, have a dance party, write a story together, or pick up a large canvas and create something beautiful. You will be surprised at how much joy and wonder you get by spending time with your Adventure Buddy. (This book is filled with ideas for things you can do with your Adventure Buddy.)

 ## Get enough sleep

Imagine this: It is Saturday morning and you have the whole day together as a family. Unfortunately, you had a long week and a hard time sleeping. Maybe the children didn't help any, waking you up for trips to the potty or a few extra tuck-ins. When they bounce into your bedroom at 6 a.m., you feel exhausted. Do you think this is a time when you will want to practice your creative thinking skills? Unlikely!

No matter how good your intentions are, without energy your efforts will become shadows of their true selves. You need sleep to be able to think clearly, concentrate, and problem solve. Additionally, lack of sleep often causes parents to be less patient and flexible—two characteristics that are required for creative thinking.

Here is our recommendation: on the day after your sleep has been poor or simply insufficient, focus on being gentle with yourself and your children. Think about ways you might get more sleep the next night, so that you will have more energy the next day. And most importantly, when you are feeling particularly tired, try to focus on being mindful with your children instead of just waiting for the day to be over.

Let go of your expectations

Before we became parents, we naively had this idea that children were blank canvases on which we could create whatever we wanted. Within a few months, we realized that our children had thoughts, passions, and views of their own. I (Cyndi) will never forget the big day we had planned to go to the pool, and all my two-year-old wanted to do was play in the car. As much as I tried to get him to come out, he was perfectly content to pretend he was a driver in the front seat. I remember feeling so disappointed, as I had this grand expectation of him jumping in the pool and swimming around with me, but that was ultimately not what he wanted. I eventually understood that it was unfair of me to have expectations of what he would or would not enjoy. I needed to let him discover and follow what he was passionate about and interested in, while at the same time exposing him to new things he could potentially enjoy.

The only way we can do this is by letting go of our expectations of what should happen. For example, you may try some of the activities in this book, and they might go over very well. Others may not. This is perfectly okay. Allow your child to be the front-seat driver when it is appropriate. You will be amazed at what you can learn!

Practice the skills we share in this book!

The skills we are sharing with you in this book aren't just for developing creative thinking in your kids. They are for you, too! As you go through each chapter, think about how the specific skill applies to you—as a person, as a professional, and as a parent. Think about how you can deliberately integrate the skill into your adult life. Try doing some of the activities on your creativity dates. Go to your local office suppy or dollar store and select a notebook that appeals to your creative senses, and journal about your experiences with the various skills. Note which skills come naturally to you, and other skills that may be more of a stretch. Remember to have an open mindset, and continue to think about how you might do things differently.

Conclusion

There is no "one size fits all" when it comes to parenting or creativity. Parenting, like creativity, is multifaceted. What works perfectly for one parent might fail spectacularly for another. We are all different people, so our parenting styles will be different. This book is filled with a variety of activities, tips, and suggestions to nurture creativity in your family. Many of them will work for you and your child, some may not. An activity may need to be modified for your child, or may even spark a different idea for an activity. Go with that! The important thing is making the space for creative thinking. (And remember, as you read, to mark the ideas you want to try out!)

As you try out the activities in this book and create experiences with your child, you will be tapping into the brilliance of the moment. Just remember that you are in the presence of an often sticky, never bored creative thinker, and let that stickiness do its magic and spark your creative thinking, too.

The skills we are sharing with you in this book aren't just for developing creative thinking in your kids. They are for you, too!

Chapter Three: The Creative Home

Making Your Home a More Creative Environment

You have probably heard the saying, "Home is where the heart is." For us, home is where the *creative* heart is—the creative heart of you and each member of your family.

No matter the size and shape of your home, you can make it the creative heart of your family. My (Michaelene's) family has lived in a variety of dwellings, from a one-room garage apartment to a spacious five-bedroom house, to a six-level tree house with piano stairs and a dragon moat (no, not really, but wouldn't that be great?). Each place we live has its own challenges and opportunities for making a creative environment. The goal is to create an environment that stimulates and nurtures creativity, a place that is comfortable and rejuvenating.

We will explore the home environment by using the metaphor of the *human* environment: the body, the mind, and the spirit. Just as these are three aspects of the human person, so too are they part of the human's home environment.

The body is the physical environment, the part of your home that can be experienced with the five senses. *The mind* of your home deals with the learning, thinking, and problem-solving opportunities that occur in the space. *The spirit* of your home is the connection you have with your family: the love, feelings of togetherness, fun, and enjoyment of life together inside the space.

Making your home a more creative environment is an excellent opportunity to engage in creative thinking as a family. The following sections will take you deeper into the three aspects of the creative home, and will include lists of questions, suggestions, and ideas that will naturally invite new and useful ideas to help foster creativity in your home.

The Creative Body

The Creative Body of Your Home: Creating the Physical Space for Nurturing Creativity

The body is the physical environment, the part of our home that can be experienced with the five physical senses: sight, hearing, taste, smell, and touch. All of the environment's physical characteristics are part of your home's body—the space, furniture, colors, temperature, lighting, and so forth.

As you and your family look for ways to make the body of your home more creative, use the five senses as a guide. Begin by asking the following questions:

★   What are all of the foods you might want to taste?

★   What sounds give you energy?

★   What scents help you relax?

★   What could you put up on the walls that would make you happy?

★   How might you make the house more colorful?

★   How could you make a cozy spot?

★   What are all of the materials you could play with?

> The spirit of your home is the connection you have with your family: the love, feelings of togetherness, fun, and enjoyment of life together inside the space.

Suggestions and ideas for nurturing the creative body of your home

★ Intentionally include all of the physical senses in your home life:

- Sight: colors, artwork, furniture, plants, lighting.

- Hearing: music, sound effects, nature sounds, friendly voices.

- Taste: new foods, taste adventures.

- Smell: food, potpourri, scented candles, scratch and sniff paper, incense.

- Touch: textures, interesting objects to touch, unique items to play with.

★ Be aware of your child's visual perspective. Often when we decorate our homes we place our images according to an adult visual perspective. Try making images accessible to your child's vantage point, placing things at their eye level as well.

★ Change things up occasionally. Rearrange furniture, try new music with dinner, put up new and interesting images, eat dinner in an unusual spot, and so on.

★ Include your child when you are thinking of ideas for ways to decorate or rearrange the house. Offer choices for how they can decorate their own room. This will help them feel connected to the physical space in your home. Use your family's artwork and creations in decorating.

★   As much as possible, make everyday living accessible to your child. Provide step stools, kid-sized cleaning and cooking tools, kid-friendly things in lower cupboards, etc.

★   Cook together. We think that cooking is magical: it involves teamwork, the stimulation of all five senses, creative thinking, problem solving—*and* it results in the creation of something wonderful (most of the time) to share with your family.

★   Go outside often. Taking the time to go outside can be a tremendous gift to give yourself and your family. There are many benefits of making a commitment to family outdoor time, including physical exercise, a deeper appreciation for nature and your community, and new opportunities for exploration, discovery, and family fun. Often we wait for good weather to go outside, but investing in good outdoor clothing such as rain boots and snow pants, and keeping old clothes to use as mud gear, will provide the comfort needed to enjoy being outside in all types of weather.

★   Create a special secluded spot for your child, a place where your child can be alone, play, think, or imagine. This spot could be a corner, tent, nook, room, closet, cupboard, or even a big brown box. Include your child when you create this space. Make it comfortable: use pillows, interesting objects, images, books, etc.

A secret space is great fun and gives your child a free space to exercise her creativity.

★ Have stuff. Make a variety of materials accessible for your child to use freely. Provide the usual materials such as paper, crayons, (safety) scissors, tape, glue, glitter, and so forth, and also provide materials that could be used in a variety of different ways, such as string, cotton balls, fabric, pipe cleaners, popsicle sticks, boxes, items that can be recycled, etc. Children have the ability to see materials in a less restrictive way than adults. As adults, we know that tape is used to stick things together. Allowing a child free access to tape, for instance, will change your view of the purpose of tape. I (Michaelene) have seen my son use tape to make armor for his action figures, a room-sized trap for any bullies that might come to our house, and temporary roads and train tracks on the carpet. Provide the materials and see what happens.

The Creative Mind

The Creative Mind of Your Home: Creating Brain Space for Nurturing Creativity

The mind of your home is made up of the cognitive, intellectual, emotional, inspirational, and learning opportunities in the environment. The mind of your home also includes the way challenges are embraced, the way new thoughts and ideas are treated, and the use of creative thinking skills on a daily basis.

As you and your family look for ways to make the mind of your home more creative, let your creative thinking skills be your guide. Begin by asking the following questions:

★ How might we learn new things as a family?

★ What are all the things we want to learn about?

★ In what ways could we make time for reading as a family?

★ How might we capture the things we are curious about?

★ What cool adventures could we take inside of the house?

★ What interesting adventures could we take outside of the house?

★ What might be all the books we want to get at the library?

★ What are all of the things we don't like in the house that we could change?

Suggestions and ideas for nurturing the creative mind of your home

★ Have a variety of reading materials accessible for your family members. This includes books, magazines, newspapers, greeting cards, instruction manuals, catalogs, maps, etc.

★ Read together every day. Even after they can read by themselves.

★ Incorporate a variety of entertainment options for your family members, being mindful of what type of stimulation these options provide. (This does not mean having 100 different television channels that enter your house through various means. This means having different types of entertainment that provide different types of stimulation.)

★ Look for the positives first when encountering new thoughts and ideas. Give positive feedback before any negative comments.

★ Treat mistakes as opportunities for learning and growing.

★ Go on family adventures.

★ Experience new things.

★ Engage in conversations.

★ Learn and share new information.

★ Ask questions.

★ Solve problems and embrace challenges together (see Skill #3, Embrace Challenges).

★ Use the Internet as a tool for learning, sharing, and exploring as a family.

★ Allow family members to follow their curiosity. If your child is interested in bugs, for instance, provide her with books, tools, new information, and experiences that nurture this curiosity.

★ Explore the natural world together.

The Creative Spirit

The Creative Spirit of Your Home: Creating the Connected Space for Nurturing Creativity

The spirit of your home is the connection you have as a family—the love, feelings of togetherness, fun, and overall enjoyment of life you have together. Oftentimes, nurturing the creative spirit of your home is as simple as spending quality time together.

As you and your family look for ways to make the spirit of your home more creative, begin by asking the following questions:

★ How could we show more appreciation for one another?

★ In what ways could we express our love for one another?

★ How might we support one another and help each other grow?

★ What might be some family rituals we could instill?

★ What might be all the ways we could have fun together?

★ What are all the things we could do for a family night?

Suggestions and Ideas for nurturing the creative spirit of your home

★ Refer to your family as a team. Name your team. Create a cheer or song together that represents your team.

★ Have a family love bracelet that each person wears that acts as a reminder that you love one another.

★ Write or draw notes to your family and post them in surprising places.

★ Engage in experiences that are fun for the whole family.

★ Schedule family game or movie nights.

★ Make family dinners more than just eating together. Use this time to talk, share, laugh, and connect.

★ Create meaningful bedtime rituals.

★ Learn together.

★ Tell stories: about your childhood, grandparents, etc.

★   Share values and beliefs as a family.

★   Volunteer together.

★   Engage in mindfulness and relaxation as a family.

★   Laugh and play together.

★   Enjoy the simple things in life together such as folding clothes, eating breakfast, and going grocery shopping.

(This page intentionally left blank...for you to draw on!)

2

Part Two: Digging Deeper

What do you wonder?
Draw pictures of things you wonder.

Skill #1: Curiosity

The important thing is not to stop questioning. Curiosity has its own reason for existing. One cannot help but be in awe when he contemplates the mysteries of eternity, of life, of the marvelous structure of reality. It is enough if one tries merely to comprehend a little of this mystery every day. **Never lose a holy curiosity.** — Albert Einstein

What is Curiosity?

Curiosity is the powerful force that drives discovery in all areas of life, from scientific findings to self-awareness. It is the internal urge to take a closer look, to experience, and to know. *Curiosity* engages the whole person: mind, body, and spirit. It drives us to look, touch, smell, taste, listen, think, feel, connect with others, and enjoy the moment.

Children are naturally and passionately curious. They are curious because they are making sense of the world. Everything is new to them, and they are driven to explore, investigate, experiment, and question. When everything is new, everything is a mystery worthy of exploration. And mysteries are exciting and compelling. Our children are like the famous explorers who shaped our human story: Carl Sagan, Steve Jobs, Ferdinand Magellan, Lewis and Clark, Calvin and Hobbes, and Alice in her Wonderland. They were, as our children are, driven by the desire to discover, that insatiable curiosity that entices our little explorers to investigate, touch, manipulate, test out, poke, engage, connect, question, search, make sense of, know, and understand. And, as adults, we have the wonderful opportunity to see the world anew as their companions on the journey of discovery.

Why is it important for creativity?

Curiosity is powerful. When it is sparked, we naturally begin to ask questions. *Curiosity* leads to *intrinsic motivation,* the internal enthusiasm that comes simply from the joy and interest of the task rather than external rewards. This leads to learning and, inevitably, *lifelong* learning. When we are curious, we want to learn more. *Curiosity* also cultivates a sense of wonder and beauty for the world we live in. Finally, it combats boredom—and sometimes arises as a result of boredom (which research shows can be a good thing).[7] We can be curious about *anything,* and we can then follow that curiosity to new experiences.

A Story

Have you ever been curious about how your child perceives the world? I (Michaelene) remember visiting Times Square in New York City for the first time with my son. He was three years old. I had seen the beautiful, vibrant, and intense frenzy of action many times before, but this was my son's first taste of Times Square. I pushed his stroller

---

7 Von Aart, J., Bartneck, C., Hu, J., Rauterberg, M., & Salem, B. (2010). How to behave as Alice in Wonderland – About boredom and curiosity. *Entertainment Computing, 1,* 125-137.

out of the subway station and into what was, to him, a whole new world. I watched his face as he took in the big picture and each new thing that caught his attention and lit his curiosity. He saw taxis, giant video billboards, and people all around. He heard music, beeping horns, and languages new to his ears. He smelled roasted nuts and summer city air. As we walked through Times Square I imagined what he was experiencing, what he was seeing. And in that moment, Times Square became new to me, too. I noticed details I would have missed. I slowed down and allowed my son to be my tour guide. His curiosity led us in our adventure, and together we discovered a whole new world.

What does curiosity look like?

Cultivate the Language of Curiosity

Use words and phrases such as:

★ I wonder...

★ That is interesting!

★ Wow! Look at that.

★ Let's take a closer look.

★ What do you notice? What else?

★ What do you think? What else?

★ What do you wonder? What else?

★ Let's explore it.

★ Great question!

★ Let's find out.

★ You are so curious!

Set the Tone!

★ Pay attention to what your child is curious about.

★ Actively wonder and think about how your child perceives the world. When you can tap into your child's perspective, you can understand your child in a deeper way.

★ Listen to, and listen for, your child's curiosity.

★ Listen to your own curiosity and follow it to new experiences and learning.

★ Listen for the real question. Sometimes when children ask "Why?" they really mean "How?"

★ Begin to ask questions about everyday objects.

★ When your child asks a question, talk about the variety of people who might have an answer. For example, "Why is hair curly or straight?" might be something to ask a hairdresser.

★ Try turning disappointments, frustrations, and challenges into things to be curious about.

★ Explore the many ways to find answers: books, the Internet, asking other people questions, doing experiments, guessing, imagining, and so on.

★ Be aware of your child's interests and ask questions related to those interests. If your child loves to use the vacuum, you might ask: What does the vacuum do? Where does the dirt go? How do you push it? What is inside the vacuum? Shall we open it up and see?

★ Don't worry about knowing the answer. The point is not for you to have the answers to all of your child's questions; the point is for you to be curious together and to find different ways to discover the answers.

★ Sometimes pretend you do not know the answers so you can discover answers together.

★ Don't rush to give an answer when your child asks "Why?" First ask, "What do you think?" Often we focus on providing answers, but allowing your child to think through his own questions can be very powerful.

★ Ask open-ended questions that do not have single answers. For example, ask, "What are all the things you see in the sky?" instead of "What color is the sky?"

★ Encourage your child to ask questions beyond the first "Why?" Not just the repetitive "why" that children ask, but "why else?"

★ Ask "What if...?" questions with your child. What if we had four legs instead of two? What if there were no stores to buy food? What if the whole world was water and there was no land?

★ When possible, create a "yes" environment: one where you do not have to say "no" too often; one where your young explorer can touch, move, change, investigate, and experience with freedom. This is more than baby-proofing the space; it is making it safe and also providing interesting opportunities for discovery.

★ Acknowledge your child's curiosity and questioning. When your child asks an interesting question, say, "That's a great question!"

> Listen for the real question. Sometimes when children ask "Why?" they really mean "How?"

Give It a Go!

★ Make a list of all the things you are curious about. Share your list with your child. Then, have your child create a list of all the things she is curious about.

★ Go on a wondering adventure. These can be elaborate day trips or simple adventures in your backyard. The key is having an adventurous attitude and intentionally allowing for curiosity and discovery to emerge. Try a wondering adventure in your neighborhood. Take a leisurely walk and allow your child's curiosity to take the lead. Walk slowly and really look, listen, touch, play, and explore.

★ Start a collection of interesting objects and bring an object out to explore on occasion. Provide the surprise of a new object and spark curiosity. You could bring out an object for your dinner table centerpiece, or secretly put a small one in your child's pocket or under a pillow. You could find something interesting for bath time or a car ride. Explore the object, ask questions, discover, and have fun.

★ If possible, have ready access to a map of the world, your country, and perhaps even your local community. Point out to your child places where relatives and friends live, places you have visited, and places you want to visit and why.

★ Take out your world map and wonder what it would be like to live in various parts of the world. Find ways (books, Internet, old encyclopedias) to go on a visual adventure.

★ Go on a library hunt. Take a question your child has and go hunt for answers in the library.

★ Have your child go through an old magazine and tear out pictures that he is curious about and likes. Create a curiosity collage.

★ Create a "Why?" day and see how many questions you can ask. Write them down and read them at dinner or bedtime. Select a few to learn about, and share what you have learned with other family members.

★ Take something apart together: an old cell phone, a hand mixer that doesn't work, a broken vacuum cleaner, etc. Learn about how it works.

★ Break things open: a flower, a seed pod, an apple, a pomegranate, a geode, a dead beetle. Wonder about what you discover.

★ When something breaks, wonder how you might fix it. Remember to be open to trying out different ideas. You may know that you can't tape a balloon back together, but allow your child to discover this.

★ Point out characters in your child's books and movies who are curious explorers. For example: Fievel from An American Tale, Alice from Alice in Wonderland, Velma from Scooby Doo, Pius Pelosi from The Room of Wonders, and, of course, Curious George.

★ Each day, go to wonderopolis.org and find the "Wonder of the Day." Discuss this with your child.

★ Create a wonder tree in your house. Make a trunk and branches and put them up on a wall. Create some blank leaves. When you or your child has a wondering, write it on one of the leaves and watch your tree grow. Periodically select wonder leaves to think and learn about.

★ Create a curiosity corner in your house. Make it a fun place for your child, and together put things in it to wonder about. Collect and display things from your wonder adventures.

Keep It Up!

★ Go to new places together and experience new things. Provide new opportunities for curiosity. Take your child to a place he has never been and point to all of the things you wonder about.

★   Explore different cultures. Wonder and learn about how different people live, play, dance, or make music, or what they eat. Make a new recipe together.

★   Wonder about the things you read in books. Learn about those things together (e.g., a book with a bat character could lead to wondering and learning more about bats).

★   Support your child's natural curiosity and provide resources for more information. When your child is curious about something, look in a children's encyclopedia, go to the library, or do a quick Internet search to find more information.

★   Wonder, think, learn, and share together: wonder about something, think about it, learn about it, then share it with others.

Use this page to draw each other's portraits.

Skill #2: Mindfulness

Living in the Present

T he most precious gift we can offer others is our presence. When mindfulness embraces those we love, they will bloom like flowers. — Thich Nhat Hanh

What is Mindfulness?

Mindfulness is being fully immersed in the present moment. It is being open and aware, while experiencing with all of our senses. When we are mindful, we are focused on the slice of life right in front of us and allowing the moment to unfold its possibilities.

Think about how you started the day. Perhaps a child was calling your name, or your alarm went off. You jumped out of bed. Checked on your child. Checked your phone. Dressed your child. Made a cup of coffee and maybe ate breakfast. Fed your child. Checked your phone again. Took a shower. Dressed yourself.

You haven't even realized it, but your day is on autopilot. This is not necessarily a bad thing; routines are useful. Imagine having to figure out anew, each and every day, how to make it through the morning's tasks. And with small children, routine provides structure and helps children feel safe. And yet, while autopilot helps us to function, it often doesn't allow us to stop, take a breath, and enjoy the moments we have.

Why is it important for creativity?

When we are mindful the mundane can become magical by adding depth to our experiences. *Mindfulness* helps us to look closely, to see things we have never seen, and to make new discoveries and connections. These skills are essential for living a creative life.

It is very easy to fall into a mindless routine, especially when leading a busy life. There are things that must be done. We shop, cook, clean, and work. We pay bills, balance the checkbook, make appointments, and drive, drive, drive. We sleep, eat, buckle the car seat, and put socks on little feet. We organize, prioritize, calendarize, and exercise.

And we wonder why we are so exhausted.

Our busy world distracts us from meaningful time with our kids, fighting for our attention. Email in our pockets turns the unimportant into the urgent. Instead, we can choose to *deliberately* and *mindfully* engage with our kids, taking much-needed breaks from the "adult world."

One of the most enjoyable aspects of developing mindfulness as a parent is the joy and authentic connection we can experience with our children. When we are mindful, the process of parenting is made deeper, more meaningful, more fulfilling, and *more frequent.*

It is essential not only for our creativity, but also for our general happiness and well-being, to slow down and notice new things, even in the most mundane tasks.

A Story

It had been a very long day at work. When I (Cyndi) arrived home, I began the nighttime routine with the kids: dinner, play, bath, story, bed. I had taken the kids to the bathroom and turned on the water. I poured the bubbles and began helping the kids get undressed. As I put them into the bath, my three-year-old yelled, "STOP!" Startled, I asked him what the problem was. He pointed out that in my mindless evening routine, I had left both of my children's socks on! As they stood in the bathtub with only socks on, we all began to laugh. And laugh. And laugh. "Socks don't go in the bathtub!" my son exclaimed. "Well today, they do!" I giggled back. This autopilot mistake gave us the opportunity to be mindful as we talked about what it was like to have socks on in the bathtub and noticed mindfully the different sensations of wet, wiggling toes.

Next time your child is in the bath, take some time to notice the little things—the softness of his hands, the shape of her toes, or even the small birthmarks on her skin. You will find when you start to notice the small things, the big picture becomes much brighter.

Cultivate the Language of Mindfulness

Use words and phrases such as:

★ What do you notice?

★ Let's take a closer look.

★ Good observation!

★ What do you see? Smell? Feel? Taste? Hear?

★ Sometimes the language of mindfulness is silence. Silence can help us focus on the present moment and shift from autopilot to observation.

Set the Tone!

★ When you are waiting in places with your child (in traffic, the post office, the grocery store line) ask your child: What do you see? What sounds do you hear? What do you smell?

★ Take the time to notice what you might overlook. Try it: put this book down and take a moment to look around the room. What do you notice? What do you smell? What do you see? What does your chair feel like? Find something in the room you haven't noticed before.

★ Take some time to mindfully observe your child. Notice how your child plays. Memorize his smile. Listen to the subtleties of her voice. Touch his hands.

★ Be a good listener for your child. When your child is sharing something with you, be sure to give your full attention and truly listen.

★ Take a mindful moment to be present with your sleeping child. Look at the shadows on your child's face, how his eyelashes rest on his cheek, notice the sound and rhythm of her breathing, and feel the warmth of soft skin.

★ Look at your child's artwork or other creations with a mindful attitude. Talk about the colors, textures, lines, etc. Talk about the feelings you have when you look at it.

★ Watch your child engage in an activity. Learn from her about how to focus your own attention. Children become joyfully absorbed in exploring. Try to find that authentic joy with them.

★ Give yourself extra time. Mindfulness is difficult when we feel rushed.

★ Practice. Mindfulness becomes easier and more natural as we practice and develop the skill.

★ Whenever possible, eliminate distractions that can prevent you from being mindful. Sometimes, put the phone away. Turn off the television. Stay with one task instead of multi-tasking. Try to say goodbye to the voice inside telling you all the things you need to get done.

★ Enjoy the simple things.

★ Make it a daily habit to be mindful at least once with your child.

★ Take time to breathe.

★ Practice relaxation exercises.

Sometimes the language of mindfulness is silence. Silence can help us focus on the present moment and shift from autopilot to observation.

What does silence look like? How does it feel?

Give It a Go!

★   If you have a pet, or could borrow a pet, take time to watch the pet's every move. "Look at Sparky's tail, how fast it can move!" "Look how long his tongue is!"

★   Take a piece of fruit and spend some time getting to know the fruit with your child. Where did it come from? How was it made? Notice if it is bruised or dented. What does it look like from the outside? What does it look like when you peel it? What does it smell like? What does it feel like in your hands? What does it feel like in your mouth? What does it taste like? What happens to it when you swallow it?

★   Stretch together and talk about how your bodies feel when you move and stretch.

★   Go outside, lie down in the grass, and stare up at the sky with your child. Take time to breathe in the air, describe the clouds, and watch the trees gently move in the breeze.

★   Take time to actually smell the roses. Pick up flowers from your local market and take the time to smell and feel each petal. Or, go for a walk at a nearby garden in a park and sit with all of the flowers.

★   Play "I spy" with your child. Look at what you spy in greater detail, using all of your senses.

★ Find a place where there are a lot of rocks, and have your child select his favorite rock. Have him take his rock in hand and give it a name. Ask your child to describe the rock to you. What does it look like? Feel like? Smell like? Tell a story of where the rock might have come from. After spending time with the rock, return it back to nature.

★ Watch a sunset together.

★ Go outside and dance in the rain (as long as there is no thunder or lightning!). What does the rain feel like on your skin? (Make sure you have towels and dry clothes ready when you come in!)

★ Make a sand hourglass. Watch the sand move back and forth.

★ Have a kitchen taste experiment. Pull out spices and other types of ingredients and taste them together. While cooking, taste each ingredient before you add it to the recipe.

★ Make up stories about a painting or other visual art piece.

★ Squish stuff: a banana, an avocado, homemade Play-Doh, pumpkin "guts," squash, etc. Don't be afraid to make a mess.

★ Play with an ice cube. Touch it and observe how it melts. Use your breath and hands to melt it. Try using a warming pack to melt it. Compare the cold with the warm.

★ In a picture book, read the pictures instead of the words. Ask your child to tell you what is happening based on the pictures.

★ Explore different textures together: use feathers, scarves, cotton balls, Q-tips, fine grade sandpaper, stickers, ice cubes, snow, grass, flowers, tree bark, tape, scouring pads, sponges, etc. Touch with hands, feet, and faces, and talk about how different parts of your bodies feel the same thing in different ways.

★ For bath time, add scented oils, bubbles, or even a few ice cubes! Use funnels, spoons, cups, and other objects, and the five senses, to explore the water.

★ Have fun with shaving cream or whipped cream: play with the cream, squish, smell, and taste it (maybe not the shaving cream). Look at the shapes of the cream and think about what those shapes look like (like cloud-gazing). Add food coloring to the shaving cream and grab a paintbrush, and you have instant paint in the bathtub that is easy to wipe away.

★ Wash dishes together. Feel the textures change as the dishes go from dirty to squeaky clean.

★ Practice mindfulness while doing the laundry. Have your child sort by color, smell the detergent (not the bleach), smell the dryer sheets, touch the warm clothes from the dryer, listen to the sounds of the washing machine and dryer.

★ Mindfully wash hands. Smell the soap, talk about how slippery your hands get, and how the water rinses the soap off. Touch each other's cheeks with your wet hands. Play with the water.

★ Find an unfamiliar park to explore. Let your child lead the way.

★ Go for long, slow walks as a family. Use all of your senses, and look for things you may not have noticed before.

> Squish stuff: a banana, an avocado, homemade Play-Doh, pumpkin "guts," squash, etc. Don't be afraid to make a mess.

★ Pick a day each week for an extra long cuddle with your child before bed. Savor every breath.

★ At dinner time each night, express gratitude for both the big things (our health, our family) and the little things (the milk we are drinking, the lady bug we managed to save and return back to nature).

Keep It Up!

★ Carve out time every day to mindfully engage with your child.

★ Take photos of your creative times together. Taking a photo naturally focuses visual attention. Print them out and put them around the house at your child's eye level or create a photo album or scrapbook.

★ Decorate your house with posters, pictures, and art pieces. Put them at your child's eye level to stimulate visual senses and begin to develop aesthetic awareness.

★ Mindfully explore new places.

★ Sit and take ten long, deep breaths together. Then, when either you or your child gets angry, try this technique to help you become calm and in tune with one another.

★ Find new ways for your family to relax together.

★ When faced with challenging situations, use mindfulness to focus, recharge and observe fully.

★ Make mindfulness a family habit.

Draw a picture of the room you are in right now.
Draw all the details you can see!

Draw a squiggle or shape, then pass the book to your partner. Have your partner draw a picture based on what you drew. If there's any room left, pass it back and add on.

Skill #3: Embrace Challenges

Becoming a Family Who Solve Problems Together

L ife's challenges are not supposed to paralyze you, they're supposed to help you discover who you are.
— Bernice Johnson Reagon

What is Embrace Challenges?

Embrace Challenges is a skill that deals with the attitudes we have when facing problems, difficulties, change, or any unfamiliar situation that does not have a clear-cut answer or way forward.

Any challenge that we encounter can be viewed in many different ways, depending on our attitudes. We can choose to view a challenge as an annoyance, a frustration, or an unnecessary stress. We can also view a challenge as an opportunity for change, a new experience, or a possibility for learning and growth. The former way is restrictive: the challenge is something to be *avoided*. The latter is more positive, proactive, and enjoyable: the challenge is something to be *embraced*.

The skill of *Embrace Challenges* requires having—or developing—the attitude of being open to challenges as opportunities for new things rather than (just) viewing them as distressing problems. Certainly, some challenges are frustrating, stressful, and annoying. The key to *Embrace Challenges* is *not* to deny the frustrations and stresses, but rather to not let these forces block you, preventing you from viewing the challenge in a more productive way.

To *Embrace Challenges,* we must first be able to *identify* a challenge when we encounter it, and then to *deliberately* choose to view it with a positive and proactive attitude. You certainly know a few adults who see every challenge as a problem to be bemoaned. These are the people who allow their negativity to affect their abilities to solve problems, and to affect the people around them. The activities we suggest for this skill are fun ways to help your child to identify and enjoy—yes, enjoy!—the opportunities that challenges bring, and to develop a positive attitude toward challenges—an attitude that will be beneficial for your child throughout life.

Why is it important for creativity?

Life is filled with challenges. Embracing the challenge at hand is the first step in being able to use creative thinking to address life's obstacles. Without this attitude, our creative thinking skills can be hindered by a pessimistic view of the challenge. Embracing it creates a positive space for creative thinking to emerge. It also helps kids become better problem solvers and work through the complexities of life—small and large—ultimately empowering them to persevere.

A Story

My (Michaelene's) mother was my first and greatest model for creative thinking. I remember many times throughout my life that I would encounter a challenge, and my mom would help me work through it from different perspectives with different types of thinking. She taught me to embrace challenges, be resourceful, persevere, pause and think about it, gauge my emotions and intuition, and problem-solve it.

I remember a project I had in my fourth grade science class. It was to build a model of the earth's rotation on its axis and revolution around the sun. I loved this project, but I made a big mistake and cut the box wrong. I was tremendously upset because I felt I had "ruined" it. My mom helped me to pause, look at what we had, think of ideas to overcome the problem, and create something that to this day I am proud of. That lesson stayed with me. I watched my mom as I grew, and when she came across a challenge, she met it with determination and creative thinking. Whether it was a family challenge, a career challenge, or an everyday we-ran-out-of-bathroom-tissue challenge, she found a way to make it work and with a positive, proactive, and creative attitude. One of the greatest gifts she gave me was the joy of embracing challenges. Today, I use the same approaches with my child.

Cultivate the Language of Embrace the Challenge

Use words and phrases such as:

★   This looks like a challenge.

★   I have a challenge for you.

★   Let's think about it.

★   Let's take a breath and look at it again.

★   I am frustrated.

★   You look frustrated.

★   This is a fun challenge.

★   I see you are working hard to overcome that challenge.

★   What ideas do you have?

Another Story

One day, I (Cyndi) picked up my son, James, from preschool and gave him a bag of old Play-Doh to play with as I cooked dinner.

"Mom, this Play-Doh is hard," he sighed to me.

Then he changed his attitude. "Mom, how might we solve this problem?" I grinned. I had been working with him on using this language when he was stuck on a problem, instead of the incessant whining that had become the norm when things didn't work.

"What ideas do you have?" I asked him.

"Well, we could go to the store and buy new Play-Doh. Or, we could go to grandma's house and ask her if she will buy me some new Play-Doh!" he exclaimed.

"We could find something else to play with," I suggested.

"We could find something else to do with the hard Play-Doh," he chimed.

Given that I had to cook dinner, we both decided we would swing by our local store after school the next day, and pick up a new pack of Play-Doh. Sometimes the non-creative response is the better one. But

Life is filled with challenges. Embracing the challenge at hand is the first step in being able to use creative thinking to address life's obstacles.

it turns out that James was not finished thinking about the hard Play-Doh he already had.

I gave James some grapes for a snack and continued to cook dinner for the family. Later, as I was about to put the food on the table, I noticed that the grapes hadn't been eaten. They had all been squished flat. Curious, I asked James what happened to his grapes.

"Mom! I took my grapes and squeezed the juice out of them. Then I poured the juice into the Play-Doh and churned it around. And then, look! I was able to make you a combine harvester!" At that point, my son proudly showed me his combine harvester which he had created from grape juice and hard Play-Doh.

"You are such a good problem solver!" I smiled at him. And I smiled for myself, too, thinking about how my son might someday teach these skills to his children.

Cultivate the Language of Embrace the Challenge—Bonus Skill: Statement Starters

Use the word "challenge" often. When challenges arise, it is very useful to phrase the challenge in a way that invites creative thinking.

The following **statement starters** will help you and your child to phrase challenges in a proactive way, and to help your family identify and embrace challenges. You and your child can then think of many different ideas to overcome the challenge and try out your ideas.

★ How to...? (e.g., How to recycle more in our home?)

★ In what ways might we...? (e.g., In what ways might we keep the bathroom clean?)

★ How might we...? (e.g., How might we spend our Friday night together?)

★ What might be all the ways...? (e.g., What might be all the ways we could get the toys back in the box without using our hands?)

Set the Tone!

★ Help your child to look at challenges in positive ways.

★ Allow your child to see you addressing challenges. Talk about what the challenge is and what you are doing to overcome it. For example, "I have a challenge! I want to make you peanut butter and jelly for lunch, but we are all out of bread! What can we do?"

★ Turn everyday tasks into fun, challenging games: getting dressed, setting the table, potty learning, table manners, brushing teeth, etc. Using a timer is a simple and fun way to do this. A challenge can be made to set the table by the time the buzzer goes off.

★ Share your feelings about challenges: your excitement, frustration, gratitude, pride, etc.

★ Re-frame tasks and chores as challenges.

★ In the midst of a challenge, talk about how it is difficult but also fun. Show your child that challenges can be enjoyable.

★ When something breaks, rather than going to buy a new replacement, try to fix it.

★ Engage in activities with your child that are slightly above your child's developmental level, activities that your child cannot do on his own. Guide your child through the process.

★ Resist the urge to solve the problem for your child. You may know the best or most efficient way to do something, but allowing your child to figure it out creates the space for discovery. Provide guidance and support when needed, and allow for curiosity.

★ Invite your child to help with the day-to-day activities of the home: shopping, cleaning, cooking, fixing/ mending, taking care of the garden, planting, washing the dishes, making grocery lists, organizing, etc. Invite your child to engage in appropriate challenges related to those tasks.

★ Be mindful of your child's emotional cues. For example, perhaps your son's body gets very rigid right before he erupts with frustration. If you learn to be aware of those changes, you can offer guidance and support in a proactive and timely way.

★   Engage in activities that show how practicing a task makes it easier. For example, putting on gloves, blowing bubbles, getting dressed, balancing on one foot.

What are some things that your child is "not old enough" to do yet...but that you might be able to let them try with supervision?

Give It a Go!

★ Hide objects around the house and have your child look for them, like an Easter egg hunt.

★ When something breaks, encourage your child to try to fix it. Make a tool box for your child that includes basic things for mending such as tape, glue, string, a tape measure, pencils, rubber bands, etc.

★ Choose a favorite board game and challenge your family to make up a new way to play it, or a new way to play with it.

★ Think about the games you played when you were a kid and share them with your child. Talk about how you played these games, and try them out with your family. Egg race, wheelbarrow race, potato sack race, hide and seek, freeze tag, tug-o-war, etc.

★ Make up a game: Give your child some random materials and challenge them to create a game to play.

★ Bring out puzzles that are slightly above your child's developmental level, and sit and put them together.

★ Scavenger Hunt Walk: Make a picture/word list of things to listen for, look for, collect, touch, etc. Then go out for a walk and have fun with the challenge.

★ Create a "Keep Trying" song. Sing it together when your child is struggling with a challenge.

★ Using cereal boxes, cut out large shapes and have your child try to put the box back together.

★ Trying new foods: When your child is reluctant to try new foods, think about framing it as a challenge. Have a taste adventure, bite, or lick something new, or go to the grocery store and look for new foods to try. Have your child choose the food to try and serve it at dinner time for the whole family.

★ Outside or in a place where you can get messy, challenge your child to move water back and forth from various objects (a bowl, a cup, a bottle, etc.). Make it a timed challenge, or have them try not to spill the water.

★ Draw maps to local destinations like the grocery store, school, grandma's house, etc. Challenge your child to follow the map as you drive or walk. Ask your child for directions.

★ Play guessing games often. Give clues to your child and invite guesses. You could give clues to places you are going, things you are going to do, or answers to questions. Example: It is hot. It is bright. It helps the grass grow. It is important for a day at the beach.

★ Learn about inventing with your child. Read books, search the Internet, and learn about inventors, inventions, and the process of inventing. Learn about the challenges that the inventor was embracing. Search the internet for Chindogu inventions (a type of Japanese inventing that will get you laughing).

Give It a Go! Bonus Ideas: Challenges

Set up challenges in your child's areas of interest. For example, if your child loves building with blocks, challenge her to build the largest tower she can and then knock it down making the loudest noise possible. Or if your child loves drawing with sidewalk chalk, challenge him to use as many colors as possible to make a drawing.

★ Listening Challenge: Take a walk and listen for different sounds. Can you hear a bird, a dog, a lawnmower, a car, music, etc.? Try making a check-off sheet to take with you.

★ Quiet Challenge: See how long you and your child can look at each other and hold hands without giggling or talking.

★ Building Challenge: Build something simple together such as a table, a flower box, a bed for your pet, a toy box, or another project. Together, draw the plans, think of ideas for materials, and construct it. The Internet has multitudes of kid-friendly project ideas.

★ Whispering Challenge: Challenge your child to a whispering game. Try whispering during bath time, dinner, playing a game, etc.

★ Setting the Table Challenge: Have your child be responsible for setting the table for each family dinner. Print out the proper table-setting configuration. Allow him to create a centerpiece. He might use clay, action figures, flowers, batteries, flashlights, or crayons.

★ "Mission" Challenge. Send your child on important missions. These missions could be to help you in some way like tidying up the house, or putting the clean laundry in the right drawers. Or these missions could be more playful, such as the Rescue Mission, to find and rescue the trapped pink kitten; or the Magic Potion Mission: she is a brave knight who needs to find the special ingredients to concoct a magic healing potion for a sick dragon. Think of fun ingredients to find: something that is shiny, something soft, something red, and something that makes you happy.

★ Cleaning Challenge: Frame the tasks of cleaning as fun challenges. How to get the dust off the ceiling fan?

★ Learning Challenges: Wonder about something and challenge the family to learn about it. Look in books, take a field trip, use the Internet, ask someone, or experiment.

★ Line Drawing Challenge: Start with a blank sheet of paper. Draw a line, shape, or squiggle and have your child continue the drawing. What could this become? Keep adding to your drawings and taking turns.

★ Treasure Hunt Challenge: Draw a treasure map for your backyard or a room in your house and "bury" a treasure somewhere. Mark the X on the map and challenge your child to find the treasure. Pretend you are pirates on the high seas! Or, go out geocaching with your smartphone or tablet to find the treasures that others have buried.

★ Finding Challenge: Find five things in the house that are...red, start with the P sound, make a noise, keep you warm, feel soft, are heavy, etc.

★ Obstacle Course Challenge: Set up an obstacle course in your house or backyard. Use the objects on hand and take turns making and running your challenging obstacle courses.

★ Sorting and Matching Challenge: Set up challenges for sorting or matching objects such as colored toothpicks, the laundry, toys, food for making a recipe, socks, etc.

★ Junk Invention Challenge: Try inventing something out of "junk" with your child. Junk can be found everywhere: things in your home that you would throw away or recycle (boxes, bottles, string, plastic bags, broken toys, old clothes, etc.) or things you find on walks. The following is a list of invention challenges to get you started. Select one of the challenges (or make up your own) and use the junk to invent something new.

- Something a superhero could use
- Something to trap and release bugs
- A robot
- A cooking invention
- An imaginary creature with special powers
- A tool to help you run faster
- A device to leap tall buildings in a single bound
- A device to make others amazed
- A toy for a pet
- A way to measure the height of an ant
- Something for a child to use to help a cranky parent
- Something to help you cool off
- Something to keep you warm
- A new kind of toy
- Something for playing in the snow
- A new musical instrument
- Dancing shoes
- Clothes
- Something to help you do your chores
- A new kind of vehicle

Keep It Going!

★   Help your child to keep embracing challenges throughout his life.

★   Allow your child to get in over his head and help him to manage the frustration of the task.

★   When challenges arise, phrase the challenge in a way that invites creative thinking: How to…, How might…, etc. (See: Cultivate the Language of Embrace Challenges–Bonus Skill: Statement Starters.)

★   Make it a family habit to look at the positives of challenging situations.

★   Highlight the opportunities that come with challenges: opportunities for more learning, fun, adventure, etc.

> Allow your child to get in over his head and help him to manage the frustration of the task.

★ Frame the other activities in this book as interesting and fun challenges.

★ Talk about challenges your child has faced and overcome through practice and perseverance, such as learning to walk, talk, use the potty, etc. When your child faces a new challenge, remind her that she has overcome challenges in the past.

★ Celebrate the courage it takes to embrace challenges.

★ Try new things together and pose them as challenges.

★ Get in the habit of addressing challenges as a family. The grownups don't have to do all the heavy lifting when it comes to creative problem solving!

Draw a picture of what your backyard looks like...
the way an ant sees it!

Skill #4: Look at it Another Way

Viewing things from Multiple Perspectives

The way we choose to see the world creates the world we see. — Barry Neil Kaufman

What is Look at it Another Way?

As parents with young children, we have likely established patterns and routines for our children. As we mentioned in the Mindfulness chapter, this is a very healthy and useful thing to do. Kids thrive in structured environments. But it's easy to fall into a pattern of doing something the same way even when it's not working, because...well, change is hard, and maybe you don't know what else to do. But doing the same thing over and over again and expecting different results can be both frustrating and exhausting (not to mention, being Albert Einstein's definition of insanity).

Look at it Another Way is about seeing things from multiple perspectives, views, or mindsets. For example, you may look at a pencil and see a writing tool. Your child may pick up a pencil and see a writing tool, a device to create a connection between toy trains, a rocket ship, or a tool to pick up his leftover Play-Doh.

To demonstrate how to *Look at it Another Way*, here's a divergent thinking[8] tool called Word Dance. With this tool, you choose a word or phrase, and then come up with many different words to describe or elaborate on it. For example, let's try this tool on the phrase "look at it another way."

Look: observe, view, see, perceive, explore, experience, delve into, glance, stare, notice, spot, glimpse, focus, watch, behold, consider, regard, study, investigate.

It: life, a challenge, a problem, an experience, parenting, mothering, playing, an object, your child, yourself, a situation, an obstacle.

Another: new, different, creative, proactive, other, an additional, further, extra, alternative.

Way: approach, manner, method, style, sense, direction, road, path.

Another Way: differently, deliberately, intuitively, in your own way.

Why is it important for creativity?

Deliberately looking at things in other ways is a simple method for encouraging our creative abilities. When we have a challenge, we shift perspective, intentionally trying to see things in multiple ways.

---

8 Divergent thinking is creating many alternatives and options. See the skill "Produce and Consider Many Alternatives" for more on this.

We go beyond what is commonplace and move into a place where the world looks different, more interesting, and full of possibility.

Looking at this in yet another way (see what we did there?), *Look at it Another Way* might just be the one thing that creative people do that people who struggle creatively do not. People who have difficulty tapping into their creativity demonstrate what's called "fixedness"—seeing certain things only one way, and being unable or unwilling to see something from any other perspective. You know fixedness when you see it—or more to the point, when you *hear* it: "I can't...," "It won't...," "You must...." It happens in politics, in PTAs, in families...and in ourselves. Embracing *Look at it Another Way* is a way of fighting against our own fixedness.

A Story

My (Cyndi's) son has always been a *very* picky eater. Whenever he was offered a new food, he would respond (politely, at least) with, "No, thank you." Following the advice of my parenting books, I would continue to offer him new foods, despite knowing what his answer would be. Sometimes, when I was desperate for him to eat vegetables, I would offer him bribes: eat the green beans, get a popsicle. (Disclaimer: this is not recommended as a parenting technique.) Some of these tactics worked some of the time.

Then, I decided to look at the problem from another perspective. I decided to have my son start cooking with me. One night, I asked him to help me make a pizza, and he was tasked with putting on the "sprinkle cheese." As he began to toss the sprinkles on the pizza dough, he would sneak sprinkles into his mouth and giggle. There I was, absolutely stunned, watching my son, who would never eat cheese, eating "sprinkles" by the handful! Now, whenever I find a food he won't try, I turn it into a sprinkle, and he usually likes it.

Next time you find that something isn't working, work with your child on looking at it from another perspective, and try to come up with new solutions.

Cultivate the Language of Look at it Another Way

Use words and phrases such as:

★   *What do you notice?*

★   *What do you see?*

★   *What else?*

★   *What is different?*

★   *Good observation.*

★   *Good eye.*

★   *Oh, I didn't notice that. Thank you.*

★   *That's interesting.*

Set the Tone!

★ Be willing to try new ways of doing things.

★ Acknowledge when something is not working and be open to other ways it could be done.

★ Try looking from your child's perspective more often. Practice what it is like to see the world from your child's viewpoint, and vice versa. Get down on your knees and follow your child around the house. What does the world look like to them? Imagine what they see, what they wonder, what they understand. It's not only fun, but it can also give you new insights into your child's behaviors and thoughts.

★ Give yourself time to observe the world.

★ Find alternative ways of doing your daily routine.

★ Listen with interest to your child's observations.

★ Help your child and yourself to look at mistakes in different ways. Mistakes are important ways for us to learn. When a mistake is made, look at it and think about what could be learned from it.

★ When a mistake is made and your child is upset, talk about what he learned, and how he could do it differently next time.

★ Whenever your child says "I don't like that," ask: "What is something you do like about it?" (e.g., "I don't like vegetables...but they make my body healthy!").

★ Look for the positives in difficult or negative situations.

★ Consider other opinions and points of view.

Give It a Go!

★ Play the game "Another Way to Say." When opportunities arise, share other words that mean the same thing. For example: delicious=yummy, sad=blue, funny=hysterical.

★ Find transparent objects in your house and begin to look at your environment with new "lenses."

★ Put your child on your shoulders and walk around. Ask them what they see from up high.

★ Lie on the floor with your child and look at the room from that viewpoint.

★ Pick an object in the house and think about all the things the object could be other than its main purpose (e.g., this toothbrush is an eyebrow, an earring, a small baseball bat).

Write the word "LOOK" below. What are all the ways you could write the word (upside down, with the o's as eyes, etc.)? Try it with other words.

★ Pick up a magnifying glass. Find objects to view through your new glass: books, nature, skin, or each other's tongues, hands, clothes, eyes, etc. What do you notice now that you didn't notice before?

★ Make glasses/a telescope/binoculars out of materials you can find in your house (toilet paper rolls, plastic drink glasses, or simply use your hands) and begin to look at things through your new set of lenses.

★ Select an object in your house and take photos of it with your child (or draw it) from as many different angles as possible. Stand on the table, crawl on the floor, do an extreme close-up. What do you notice?

★ Select a room in your house that you could change. Move the chairs, toys, anything to change perspective. What do you notice when sitting in a different spot?

★ Make shadow puppets with your hands. What might your hands become?

★ In the car, hang a picture off the back of the front seat, facing your child. Ask him to describe what he sees in the picture. The next day, move the picture so it is upside down or sideways, and ask him to describe what the picture looks like from that angle.

★ Read a book from the last page to the first page. Ask: what did you notice when we read it that way?

★ Go to the playground and look at things from different vantage points. What does the hat on the ground look like from the top of the slide? From the inside of the sandbox?

★ Choose a flower, bush, or tree in your backyard or neighborhood. Take a photograph of the plant on the same day each month. What does it look like as it changes through each season?

★ Pick up some cellophane at your local grocery store. Look at things through pieces of different colored cellophane.

★ Select a doll or animal toy and talk about where the toy came from, what the toy sounds like, what it might like to eat, etc.

★ Give your child a kaleidoscope.

★ Play with small toys in different ways: dinosaurs in the dryer, motorcycles in the kitchen sink, construction vehicles under the dining room table.

★ Grab a few flashlights and turn off all the lights. Then, observe what the house looks like in the dark.

★ Take a glass of water and talk about all the things you can do with it (freeze it, boil it, make cocoa with it, etc.).

★ Choose a favorite animal and look for it in your various children's books. How does it look in each story?

★ Pretend you are an alien visiting Earth for the first time. Ask your child questions about the world. Have your child explain what things are and how things work. Enjoy being a tourist on Earth.

★ Look at dinner in a different way: Eat dinner by candlelight, have breakfast for dinner, make a color-themed dinner, play with your food, make creations with your food and eat them, have a picnic on the floor, eat under the table, eat without utensils.

★ Whenever you come across a new animal or insect with your child, imagine what it must be like to be that creature.

★ When the seasons are changing, look for signs of the new season. In spring the robins come back, the buds get bigger on the trees, you hear birds singing, etc.

Keep It Going!

★ Look for ways to reuse objects. Begin to save things from your recycling bin. Every time you or your child go to put something into the bin, ask, "What else could we make with this object?" For example, maybe your old cereal box turns into a garage for toy cars, or the start of a play house.

★ Take a family picture in the same position once every year. As the years pass look at how each of you has grown and changed.

★ When family disagreements arise try to look at the situation from each person's perspective.

★ When something is not working, look for new alternatives.

★ When challenges and problems arise, look at them in different ways.

★ As a family, embrace mistakes and failures as opportunities for new learning and growth.

★ Encourage your family to remain open-minded to new people and situations.

★ Embrace the diversity of people. Create opportunities to explore and understand how different people live throughout the world.

What are all the things this could be?

Skill #5: Produce and Consider Many Alternatives

Going Beyond One Right Answer

When you've exhausted all possibilities remember this: you haven't. — Thomas Alva Edison

What is Produce and Consider Many Alternatives?

If variety is the spice of life, then *Produce and Consider Many Alternatives* is the well-stocked spice cabinet. There are many ways to think about and do things. Our educational systems are based on the premise that there is one "correct" answer to a question. For some questions, certainly, this is true. However, most of life's issues, situations, and quandaries do not have one "right" answer.

This skill is about going beyond the first response, answer, idea, or option, and exploring a variety of possibilities that might be one's own right answer.

Why is it important for creativity?

When faced with opportunities or challenges, we often jump to the first option that comes to mind. But when we take time to think of a variety of options, we are able to go beyond the obvious, to find new and useful possibilities. This is the creativity skill that allows us to go beyond the initial taste, to find new flavors and possibilities.

A Story

Some time ago I (Michaelene) took my son to the doctor because he had a sore throat. Everything was fine at first; we looked at the fish in the aquarium, read a few books. Then came the dreaded strep throat test, in which a kind nurse sticks an unkind, oversized Q-tip down the throat to get a sample. Understandably, my son freaked out. Even after the sample had been taken, he was still very upset. Knowing my son, I knew that if I gave him a good challenge to think about he would focus on it and it would help him calm down. I said, "You have really good ideas. What inventions can you think of to make a strep throat test better for kids?" My young inventor came up with a variety of new inventions including a popsicle strep test, a way to just lick the swab, a feather test, and a spitting test. As he thought of many different possibilities, he calmed down and we even giggled a bit.

Cultivate the Language of Produce and Consider Many Alternatives

Use words and phrases such as:

★ This could be...

★ What if...?

★ What else...?

★ How else...?

★ Where else...?

★ Who else...?

★ Why else...?

★ Why do you think...?

★ Let's try it a different way.

★ What might be all the ways...?

Set the Tone!

★ When your child is faced with a challenge, take some time to help him think of multiple ideas to overcome the challenge.

★ When your child has an open-ended question, help her to think of multiple possible answers.

★ Be willing to experiment with new ways of doing things. Experimentation can sometimes be messy, ambiguous, and not always successful. The important element with this skill is to try to think and take action in a variety of ways.

★ Postpone your judgment of new ideas and options. Often new possibilities are limited by our initial judgments. (This is a hard one! But very, very important for creativity.)

★ Strive for many options. Stretch your thinking past the first few ideas or options. Have fun with thinking of new ways to do and create things.

★ Embrace the silliness that can come with new ideas and options.

Try out the "why else" question here.

Why do dogs bark? Write down one answer.
Then ask—and keep asking—why else do dogs bark?
Don't stop with "real" answers. Fill the page with ideas!

Give It a Go!

★ Play with safe non-toys in the house. To a preschooler, a spoon can become many different things: a shooter, a shovel, a spaceship, a tuba, a fountain, a robot arm that fell off, buried treasure, a fire hose, or a creature. Find different playful uses for everyday objects.

★ Pick two objects in your house (e.g., a ball and some string) and invent new games to play.

★ Listen to different variations of a song with your child. Show how there can be a variety of ways to play and sing the same song. Compare and contrast the different variations of the song. Talk about what sounds are different and similar. Try making your own version of the song together.

Postpone your judgment of new ideas and options. Often new possibilities are limited by our initial judgments.

★ Select an object for the day (toilet paper roll, sippy cup, ball, etc.) and think about all the uses it could have as you go through your daily routine.

★ Make multiple copies of a picture from a coloring book and try coloring the pictures in a variety of ways, or using a variety of materials: crayons, markers, pens, paints, mud, berries, etc.

★ Choose a favorite food, then prepare and eat it in a variety of ways. Example: Bananas can be peeled from the top or bottom; sliced into circles or strips; mashed up; and made into smoothies, pudding, muffins, bread, and many other delicious concoctions.

★ Select a favorite animal and create it with as many different materials as you can find. Make different variations: one with Play-Doh, one with Cheerios, one with pasta, one with "junk," etc. Or you could use a variety of materials to make one animal, e.g., with Play-Doh legs, Cheerio eyes, and pasta whiskers.

★ Build things with marshmallows and uncooked spaghetti. Explore the many different things that can be constructed with marshmallows and spaghetti: towers, castles, robots, spiders, tents, a marshmallow family, spaceships, etc. Have fun discovering new ways to use these and other edible materials.

★ Buy a roll of masking tape for your child. (Painter's tape works especially well, and it's blue!) Play with and explore the many ways to use masking tape. Fix things, make faces with the tape on each other's shirts, make finger puppets, invent a game using tape balls, make a road for toy cars, write words and label things in your house, make a costume, etc.

★ Help your child get dressed in a different (and silly) way. Put socks on the ears, pants on the head, a shirt on backwards, and then try new silly combinations.

★ Take a brand new story and read the first line. Then ask your child, "What are all the things that could happen next?"

★ Go to the swimming pool and try to move through the water in different ways. What are all the ways you can enjoy the water?

★ Get a Frisbee and think about all the different ways you can use it.

★ Using a drawing of your child's hand, think about all the things the hand could become (a turkey, a flower, an octopus, the sun, etc.).

★ Have a silly sock day. Think of all the ways you might make your socks silly! Create your socks, have a fashion show, and wear them out for the day.

★ While grocery shopping, ask your child what might be all the things she could eat for lunch, dinner, or snack.

★ Explore different ways to clean up toys: use hands, use feet, clean slowly like a snail, or quickly like a cheetah, or clean up by color (all of the red toys first).

★ Read different versions of the same story. Fairy tales, folk tales, and nursery rhymes work well for this. "The Three Little Pigs" is a good place to start, as there are many different books that tell this classic tale. Compare and contrast the pictures and words from each book. Try making your own versions of classic stories.

★ On Friday night, have a family brainstorm of all of the things you could do over the weekend.

★ Take different routes to common places: the store, school, playground, etc. Explore the many different ways and paths that can be taken to get to the same place.

★ Try different modes of transportation: walking, riding bikes, driving, public transportation, skipping, piggy back rides, etc.

★ Save, play with, and make things from boxes or other recyclable materials. For example, your old shoebox could make great robot feet or a treasure chest.

Keep It Going!

★   Make a rainy day activity jar. With your family, think of many different possibilities for indoor activities that could be done on a rainy day. Write or draw a picture of each activity on a slip of paper. Add to the jar as you think of new activities. On a rainy day, select an activity and enjoy.

★   When your child encounters an obstacle (e.g., a ball rolls under the couch, food falls on the floor), have him think of a variety ways to overcome the obstacle (get a broom, use a toy to retrieve the ball, etc.).

★   Start a "junk" box, and fill it with items and objects that could be used in different ways. These objects could be things in your home that you would throw away or recycle or even random "treasures" you find on walks. Keep adding items to the box and use the objects to make new things such as art pieces, gifts, crafts, toys, and imaginary inventions.

★   When you are solving problems as a family, take time to think of many possible solutions to your challenge.

★   As your child grows and asks more in-depth questions, make it a habit to search for a variety of answers in a variety of places (in books, videos, experts, etc.).

★ As your child enters more formal educational settings, be sure to reinforce that there can be many different ways to do things (such as solving a math problem, studying spelling words, or writing a story) and many possible answers to open-ended questions.

What can you do outside on a rainy day?
Draw a picture or make a list.

What does play look like to you?

Skill #6: Playfulness

Play energizes us and enlivens us. It eases our burdens. It renews our natural sense of optimism and opens us up to new possibilities. — Stuart Brown, MD

What is Playfulness?

It doesn't seem as if we need to ask this question, but let's ask it anyway, for curiosity's sake: When we talk about play, what do we mean?

Stuart Brown said, "Play is an ancient, voluntary, inherently pleasurable, apparently purposeless activity or process that is undertaken for its own sake and that strengthens our muscles and our social skills, fertilizes brain activity, tempers and deepens our emotions, takes us out of time, and enables a state of balance and poise."[9]

Why is it important for creativity?

Play is a powerhouse. It provides physical, mental, emotional, and social benefits. When it comes to creative thinking, *Playfulness*

---

9 http://www.journalofplay.org/sites/www.journalofplay.org/files/pdf-articles/1-4-interview-importance-ofplay-stuart-brown.pdf

allows us to engage in imagination; explore and toy with thoughts, ideas, and possibilities; have a more optimistic perspective; harness intrinsic motivation; make mistakes and bounce back; and engage in problem solving.

One of the more interesting things about play is that it provides these benefits for all people, not just for children. (Yes, parents, we're talking to you!)

Playfulness is a natural state for children. And while it seems as if it's all fun and games, children are working hard when they play. In play, children make decisions, prioritize, gain and use knowledge, develop strengths and skills, and face and overcome challenges.

Play can be more challenging for adults. Often as we get older, playing becomes something we indulge in after the work is done...and often the work is never done. As we continue maturing, we tend to focus more on what is real, efficient, necessary, and "important." That tight focus alone can rob us of the joy found in the small, silly, and precious moments of life. And on those days that are stressful and overwhelming, being with your child can be a beautiful break from the real-world worries and challenges, a time when you can put aside the stresses and, for that moment, make play your sole responsibility and goal. This can be a meaningful gift you give to yourself and your child. You will be amazed at what you learn from your resident play expert!

A Story

Going to the grocery store is never an easy task for my two kids and me (Cyndi). They can be perfectly fine one minute, and the next, one is hitting the other with bananas or dropping tomatoes out of the cart to watch them roll, while the other is having a complete meltdown over not being able to hold the cookie box. This is difficult and frustrating in and of itself. However, I am always amazed at the comments and "words of wisdom" I get from other people at the grocery store when this occurs. "Why is she crying?" or "Don't worry, you will get through this," or my personal favorite, "Small kids, small problems. Wait till they get bigger!"

On one particular Saturday, when I needed to get a great deal of food for a family party, we reached the final aisle of the grocery store when the bickering started. My daughter launched into a full blown hysterical meltdown in the middle of the aisle. To make matters worse, I had my mother-in-law in from out of town, and she was looking at me with gentle desperation. The comments from the passerby shoppers began, and I was about to lose it.

I didn't feel we could just walk away from the situation, as we had a cart full of groceries I had to have for the special meal I was preparing. Plus, I was on a time constraint. I needed to get through the checkout line. As I pulled up to the checkout, my daughter continued to sob, and I began to throw the groceries onto the conveyer belt. My mother-in-law asked me sweetly, "What about the coffee?" I sent her off to find it so we could get out of there as fast as we could.

Just then, an elderly woman, maybe mid-80s, came into the line behind me. She looked at me and my children with sympathy, and I braced myself for another comment.

Instead, she bent over to my children to get their attention. "Did you see the puppy in the grocery store?" she asked them. Immediately, my daughter stopped crying, and my son stopped trying to swindle a Twix bar. All attention was on her. "Puppy?!" my son asked. "Yes, puppy. Listen!" Just then, the elderly woman turned her head so the children couldn't see her face, and began to bark. They started to giggle. She turned back around. "Did you hear it?" Both children nodded with delight. She spun her head around again. "Woof! Woof!" She came back to us and said, "Oh no! He is running away! Woof! Woof!"

After the reenactment of the running puppy, my kids had calmed down, and we made it through checkout. I thanked the elderly woman for her kindness and help.

"I was married a long time, and I had five kids," she explained to me. "The one thing I learned in my life is that you need to have a sense of humor." Words of wisdom that I will never forget.

> Play is a natural state for children. It can be more challenging for adults.

Cultivate the Language of Playfulness

Use words and phrases such as:

★ That's funny.

★ You are so funny!

★ You are so silly!

★ This is fun!

★ Let's play!

★ What would you like to play?

★ I love playing with you.

★ You are good at playing.

★ You crack me up!

★ I love your sense of humor.

★ I love the sound of your laugh.

Set the Tone!

★   Carve out time for free play. Don't put an agenda or goal to it. Allow your child to lead the play.

★   Allow for more laughter. Sometimes we can forget, in the midst of a hectic day, to laugh a little.

★   Point out things that you find funny to you in order to increase your child's awareness of humor.

★   Remember to take every opportunity to smile and laugh with your child.

★   Enjoy your child's laugh every time you hear it.

★   Be deliberately playful.

★   Try playing with your child and reflecting on your experience. What did it feel like to play? How did your child respond to your playful attitude?

★   Allow yourself the time and space to be spontaneous on occasion.

★   Share funny observations with your family.

★   Look for ways to bring playfulness to other areas of your life. Be gentle with yourself. Some days it is hard to find the humor in difficult situations.

Think about your attitudes and values around play.
How do you view play?

Is there anything that stops you from being playful?

Give It a Go!

★ Make a list with your child of things that you find silly, playful, or humorous.

★ Make a list of fun and silly things to do on a rainy day, or any day.

★ Make a list of the people who make you laugh in your life, and make plans with them regularly.

★ Try all the different ways to laugh: giggle, snicker, belly laugh, laugh like a villain. Ask your child how a monkey would laugh, or a shark, or a robot. Have fun inventing new ways to laugh.

★ Record the sound of your child's laugh and play it for him, or make it your ringtone.

★ Take a trip to the dollar store and find some things that could make your child laugh. For example, big clapping hands, a red clown nose, gigantic sunglasses.

★ Engage in hide and seek games. When you are hiding, find a way to use the items from the dollar store.

★ Make a treasure map of your living space. Have your child try to find a "treasure" by searching on the map.

★ Point out incongruities, puns, things that are funny, and words that sound silly together.

★ Make up silly songs to everyday activities. For example, "Wouldn't it be groovy to make a blueberry-banana-vanilla-cream smoothie?"

★ Draw smiley faces on paper and put them all over the house at your child's eye level.

★ Read silly song lyrics and poetry books. Sing silly songs. Make up your own silly songs, raps, and poems.

★ Sing songs deliberately out of tune together.

★ Make up new words to bedtime stories. For example (from Goodnight Moon), "In the great blue room, there was a hippopotamus and a grand cartoon..."

★ Make breakfast/lunch/snack time fun and different, and surprise your child: cut up his sandwich into different shapes, make a fruit or vegetable robot/building/etc., make a waffle house, or make something out of a napkin.

★ Turn the wall hangings in a room upside down or rearrange the furniture.

★ Do something funny to your appearance before you walk into the room: put stickers all over you, wear your hair in a funny way, wear a clown nose.

★ Dinnertime fun: Eat dinner in a strange place: under the table, in bed, outside, under a blanket tent. Eat dinner with just your hands. Feed each other. Set the table in a different way.

★ Play with balloons: bat them around, blow them up and let them go shooting off, keep the balloon from touching the ground, use static electricity to stick a balloon on a wall. Fill a room with balloons and play with them. (Please remember to be very careful with balloons and very young children!)

★ Play in the snow together. Build a snow fort. Make snow angels. Make snow aliens. Make your family as snowmen.

★ Draw silly pictures of your family.

★ Play the "What if" game: What if the furniture was made of spaghetti? What if our pet could fly?

★ Create funny food concoctions.

★ Play with Play-Doh, a fantastic creativity toy. Make your own Play-Doh together.

Draw and color a balloon, or a whole lot of balloons!

★   Tell jokes and funny stories.

★   Tell each other jokes. Teach your child about knock-knock jokes. Explain jokes.

★   Dress in crazy outfits and take a photograph.

★   Slapstick comedy: play with slapstick humor. Watch slapstick movie clips such as The Marx Brothers, The Three Stooges, Flubber, and Charlie Chaplin movies.

★   Get magnets to "jump" together.

★   See how long everyone can keep a straight face while doing silly things.

★   Make silly noises. Take turns to make the silliest noise you can think of.

★   Stage a comedy show with all of your stuffed animals.

★   Practice laughing meditation. Lie down with your child on the floor touching hands and just laugh together as hard as you can. Start by fake laughing, and that will turn into real laughter.

★   Use a camera app and make funny faces and poses.

★ Bring a straw into the bath and see how many bubbles you can blow. (Make sure not to swallow any bathwater!)

★ Have the products in your shopping cart talk to each other.

★ Take your kids "park hopping."

★ Give your child a bin full of old toys and ask him to create a game with you. Let him take the lead!

★ When having a rough day, find a movie that will make you laugh. (We strongly recommend "Parenthood." If you haven't seen it since becoming a parent, you're in for a treat. But watch it while your child is napping.)

★ Make sock puppets.

Keep It Going!

★ Once a month, create a day of little surprises. For example, chocolate chips in pancakes, a special photograph found underneath the pillow, a trip to a new park, a visit with a special friend.

★ Have a Family Laugh Night: tell jokes and funny stories, watch a funny movie, play games without using the directions.

Draw a silly family portrait.

★ Take a silly family photo. Send it out as a greeting card. Put it up on the wall.

★ Make silly hats, and wear them when you want to be silly, crazy, etc. This could also help with keeping the super-crazy-silliness in context.

★ Have an annual FUN Party!

★ Create a journal of "someday, these will be funny" stories about parenthood. (How do you think we came up with the stories in this book?)

★ Find funny cartoons, sayings, pictures, or quotes and put them up in your house, car, or workspace.

★ Make family fun an important part of your life.

Turn on your favorite song and draw a picture
to the music!

Skill #7: Make it Swing! Make it Ring!

f you can walk you can dance. If you can talk you can sing.
— Zimbabwe Proverb

What is Make it Swing! Make it Ring!?

Make it Swing! Make it Ring! is about experiencing, responding to, and using movement, sound, and song to express yourself and to explore the world around you. It is using kinesthetic and auditory senses: listening, dancing, singing, moving, making noises, swaying, gesturing, acting out, mimicking, and enjoying the movement of the body and the experience of sound.

Why is it important for creativity?

Creative thinking is a whole-body experience. We think, embrace challenges, and experience the world with our brains, our bodies, and our voices. This skill taps into the body as a vehicle for creative thinking and expression.

A Story

Advice is never in short supply when you are pregnant. When I (Cyndi) was pregnant with my son, my family and friends were a constant source of parenting anecdotes, and some of the stories even proved to be true! But one thing no one ever mentioned was the singing. As soon as I brought my son home from the hospital, I found that almost every interaction became a song.

"We're going up the stairs, we're going up the stairs, hi-ho the derry-o, we're going up the stairs!"

"We're getting in the car, we're getting in the car!"

You may have noticed that these songs were actually rather contrived versions of "The Farmer in the Dell," not quite original compositions. But the point is that setting our actions to music made intuitive sense to me, and once my son started talking, he began to sing, too.

Why do we sing to our children? Because it's fun! Setting movement to music and playing with sound energizes us and offers a different way to think. We have used made-up songs to teach things ranging from our home address to the importance of applying diaper rash cream when needed. And it is amazing to see how these songs, some of them five years old, continue to stick in our heads!

Cultivate the Language of
Make it Swing! Make it Ring!

Use words and phrases such as:

★   Did you hear that?

★   It sounds like...

★   Listen, what do you hear?

★   That's an interesting sound!

★   This is a great song!

★   Let's dance!

★   Let's sing!

> Creative thinking is a whole-body experience.

Set the Tone!

★ Sing songs together, even if you are completely out of tune. (Don't worry about how your voice sounds. Your singing will be awesome to your child!)

★ Don't get caught up in having to have all of your songs rhyme.

★ Enjoy the silliness!

★ Don't be afraid to let loose. It is okay if you can't move well—just try!

★ Look for ways to use sound, song, and movement in your daily life.

Give It a Go!

★ Experiment with different ways to move. Walk, run, dance, move like a _____ (robot, elephant, cat, rabbit, frog...).

★ Teach your child your address or phone number by creating a song with hand motions.

★ Try creating the ABCs with your body.

★ Have a dance party. Turn on different types of music and dance together. If you want to make it a very special activity, you could make invitations, decorate, dress up, make punch, or use a colored light bulb.

★ Blow bubbles and experiment with different ways to pop the bubbles: pinching, clapping, kicking, stomping, moving slowly, etc.

★ Listen to all of the different sounds your car makes. Try to recreate them.

★ Create a name and voice for your car. What does your car say while you are driving?

★ When outside, listen to the sounds the birds make. Listen for the differences in sound. Try to mimic the bird sounds. Imagine what kind of songs are they singing. Create your own bird song.

★ Teach your child the words to your favorite song.

★ In your home, post the lyrics to a song your child loves. Invite your child to draw a picture to go along with the words.

★ Make up an "I love you song" for your child, and sing it to her often.

★ Create a dance, such as a special celebration dance or happy dance.

★ Create a secret handshake that no one outside the family can know.

★ Talk to your child through the heating/cooling vents in your house. Explore how sound travels through the ventilation ducts.

★ Get a towel and lay it out in the house. Have your child lie down, close his eyes, and pretend he is at the beach. Play beach music with crashing waves, and ask him to describe what he hears. (This activity is especially good for cold days!)

★ Spend a day trying to turn everything into a song.

★ Walk through the house and explore the many ways to make sounds: knocking on the door, opening and closing the cupboard, etc.

★ Make up songs together. It is helpful to use a familiar melody and add your own lyrics. You could create a family song, a waking up song, a dinnertime song, a going-to-school song, a bathtub song. (One of my son's favorites is sung to the old Batman theme song: "Ba-ba, ba-ba, ba-ba, ba-ba, bathtime! Bathtime!")

★ Select your favorite book, and try to reenact it with only your body. Then try to create a song about it.

★ Point out vibrations you notice. Listen to and feel the vibrations. Talk about how sound is a vibration of the air. Conduct some vibration experiments.

★ Learn about different musical instruments together: read books, search the Internet for videos with different instruments, or take a trip to your local music store or school. Listen to the variety of sounds the instruments make, and talk about what they sound like to you and your child. What feeling in your body do you get by listening to each instrument?

★ Search the Internet for different types of music videos. Look for kids playing instruments.

Create a secret handshake. A happy dance. An "I love you" song.

★ Use your voice as an instrument. Pretend to be a guitar, a drum, a harmonica, etc.

★ Make instruments together. Try making a drum, maracas, a tissue box guitar, a rain stick, etc.

★ Create a marching band parade with your family. Use real instruments or pretend instruments. Make a flag. March around your house or neighborhood.

★ Improvise changes in lyrics of songs your child knows. Start singing the song and have your child fill in the next word. For example: "The itsy-bitsy __ (dragon, turtle, bird, superhero, robot, princess, stickle-back fish...) crawled up the water spout...", "Yankee Doodle went to _____ (the grocery store, Grandma's House...) riding on a ____ (doughnut, rocket ship, airplane, fruit fly...)." Don't worry about it rhyming or making sense. Be silly! (This needs to be modeled first a few times.)

★ Sing a favorite book together to the tune of a favorite song.

★ Clap, snap, pat, and stomp out different patterns of rhythms together. Mimic each other's rhythms. Add on to each other's rhythms.

★ Make up a song about challenges. Or use one that you find (Yo Gabba Gabba has a "keep trying" song). Sing this song when your child is encountering a challenge.

★ Next time it is raining, listen to what the rain sounds like. Then create a rainstorm, making the sounds with your voice and body (snaps, rubbing hands together, stomping on the floor, tapping on the window, etc.).

★ Get some PVC pipes from your local home improvement store. (Take your child with you. We've yet to meet a child who doesn't love a hardware store.) Cut the pipes to different lengths. Tap, pound, and play with the tubes using different things: hands, spoons, drumsticks, etc. Make music and sounds together.

★ Set up pots and pans like a drum kit, and have a jamming session.

★ Watch the movie or theater production "Stomp" with your child. Then look for ways to "stomp" your house, making music in unusual ways.

★ Create a Pandora music list together. When you listen to a song, ask your child whether they liked it or not (and click on the thumbs up or down on Pandora).

★ Make your child a CD as a gift, like the mixtapes of old. Include some of your favorite songs, songs your child knows, and some new songs.

Keep It Going!

★ Teach through movement. Act out the things you are learning about together: a seed growing into a tree, the sun rising, shining, and setting, the water cycle (rain falling, becoming a puddle, evaporating, forming a cloud, and falling again), a volcano erupting.

★ Create a playlist of music that you and your child love.

★ Designate time each day to physically stretch with your child.

★ Listen to the sounds around you. Describe what you hear with your child. Point out how some noises could sound like music, and listen for rhythms. Try listening to the music of the washer and dryer, the songs of nature, the symphony of the city, the rhythms of the garbage truck, or the beat of the supermarket.

★ Read, sing, and rap poetry for your child.

★ Sing directions you want your child to follow. Sing questions and answers with your child. Sing short descriptions of what you see, hear, taste, touch, smell.

★ When you hear an interesting sound, share it with your child.

★ Go to a parent and child music class together.

★ Go to community music events together.

★ Expose your child to a variety of music: show tunes, jazz, classical, swing, hip hop, bluegrass, aboriginal drumming, salsa, rock and roll, old school country, folk, Gregorian chant, Native American, world music...

★ Be aware of your child's musical interests and provide more opportunities for exploration.

★ Set up a music center with a variety of instruments: harmonica, drums, recorder, maracas, bells, etc.

★ Make movement for enjoyment a family habit.

★ Learn sign language together and use it as another way to communicate.

★ Think back to the songs you learned in your childhood and share them with your child.

★ Make music an important part of your home and life.

Sing things. Sing directions, questions and answers, or just about anything.

Draw a picture with your child that includes
every color crayon that you own!

Skill #8: Visualize It Richly and Colorfully

The real voyage of discovery consists not in seeking new landscapes but in having new eyes. — Marcel Proust

What is Visualize It Richly and Colorfully?

After you read this paragraph, close your eyes and imagine your favorite food. Think about the rich and beautiful colors of the food. Pretend to touch and explore the textures of the food. Smell the aroma that ensues. Imagine taking a big bite of your favorite food and savor the taste.

Visualize It Richly and Colorfully is about using and creating imagery that stimulates and inspires our senses, creating vibrant pictures in our minds.

In completing the exercise above, you might have experienced a mental tickling of not only your visual sense, but of all of your senses! Engaging our senses is an essential component toward building our creative thinking skills.

Why is it important for creativity?

When faced with potential opportunities or challenges, being able to *Visualize It Richly and Colorfully* provides us with a larger spectrum of sensations to draw upon. When we tap into this spectrum, we can imagine and express our thoughts, ideas, and goals in a deeper, richer, and more meaningful way. It is like having a box of 64 crayons to draw with, versus a box of only 8 crayons... with the built-in sharpener, too.

A Story

"Mom, I'm not hungry," my (Cyndi's) four-year-old son declared one morning at breakfast.

"Why not, my love? Are you feeling okay?" I questioned.

"Oh, I feel fine, I just ate a lot last night with Patrick John in Fridayland."

This was not the first time we had heard about Patrick John, my son's imaginary friend. In fact, almost every day we heard about the nighttime visits to Fridayland to spend time with Patrick John. Just a quick prompt of "Tell me more about that" led him to a soliloquy describing his vision of what he saw in his imaginary dream world.

"Fridayland is a place where it's Friday every day, and they only serve vanilla ice cream with rainbow sprinkles on top! Patrick John lives there with his parents, Vaprick John and Haprick John in a three-hundred-thousand-foot house that often smells like chicken wings!

He is five thousand one hundred million years old, about two hundred feet tall, and has a very long white beard. When we are together, we like to create our own experiments, like taking two umbrellas with Lego in-between, and seeing what happens when it rains, and what might get wet."

Cultivate the Language of Visualize It Rich and Colorfully

Use words and phrases such as:

★ What colors do you see?

★ What does it feel like?

★ What does it smell like?

★ What are the textures?

★ Describe to me...

★ Give me more details.

★ I can picture it in my mind.

Set the Tone!

★ Point things out and describe things in detail by color, size, and texture. For example, "Look at that oval, turquoise-and-purple pillow. It looks so soft!"

★ Don't be afraid to get messy.

★ Don't have expectations of what something should or should not look like.

★ Embrace imperfections.

★ Participate with your child.

★ Ask your child a lot of open-ended questions to help uncover their ideas.

★ When telling a story or sharing how your day was, describe the details.

Give It a Go!

★ Pull out a big box of crayons and talk about the different colors in the box. Explore the hues of each color. Which crayons are blue, which are light blue? How is each color created?

★ Create a rainbow from colored objects in your house.

★ Pick a color of the day and identify all the items you see with that color.

★ Take your child for a walk and notice all of the different textures that you see.

★ Get a prism and begin to explore the colors you see.

★ Start a store color mission. Every time you go shopping, your child has to find five things in one specific color.

★ Make a trip to the art store and have your child pick out a special paintbrush and colorful art supplies.

★ Get non-toxic finger paints. Don't be afraid to get messy—just be prepared with old clothes, and get the bath ready! Put out large sheets of paper or buy white canvas and allow your children to use their hands, feet, elbows, and knees to paint. Hang your painting in the house.

★ Create a family painting.

★ Create a color from mixing paint. Name the color after your child.

★ Imagine a purple frog, a blue turtle, and a pink cow. Have your child come up with colors for various animals.

★ Create colored glasses from colored cellophane. Ask your child what the world looks like in that color.

★ Make black and white photographs and have your child add color.

★ Change the color balance of your TV. What does it look like with a green screen? With a yellow screen?

★ Take a trip to the art museum, and focus on one colorful piece of art. What does your child see? What colors are in the picture?

★ Create color names. "This looks like ostrich pink!"

★ Get a flashlight and put a colored shell over it. Turn out the lights. What does the kitchen look like when you view it in red? Blue?

★ Have a contest on who can create the most colorful outfit. The winner gets rainbow sherbet ice cream.

★ Make a collage about your child, your family, the seasons, or your wishes, or tell a story through collage.

★ Look at comic books together. Pay attention to how the artist uses images to tell the story.

★ Ask your child to imagine what he will look like when he is grown up, and have him draw a picture.

★   Go through a cookbook or cooking website and have your child select something that looks appealing. Cook the meal together.

★   Ask your child to imagine the best tasting milkshake. What would go into it? Create the milkshake with your child. (It's OK if it tastes terrible!)

★   Make a grocery list using pictures, and get your child to help you find the items on the list.

★   Make your own "Technicolor Dreamcoat" from old clothing. Make it with all of your favorite colors.

★   Have your child select her favorite color and make it the "Color of the Month." Create a sign with that color, make cards, and have everyone in the family wear clothes of that color. Make a special cake with that color frosting. See if there are any library books with the color as the title, and borrow them. Make this an annual tradition on a specific day each year.

★   When shopping, describe what you are looking for in a riddle. For example: It comes in bunches, it is curved, it is yellow on the outside, it tastes sweet, monkeys like to eat it.

★   Once a month, try to make a monochromatic dinner: all white foods, purple, orange, etc. Or, try to make a rainbow dinner!

★   Read books without pictures. Have your child close his eyes and use his imagination to create the pictures.

★   Once a month, create lunches with all of the same shaped food. For example, triangular sandwiches, carrots in the shape of triangles, etc.

Draw a rainbow that no one has ever seen before.

Keep It Going!

★ Expand your child's descriptor vocabulary by using new words often, including words above their age level.

★ Practice noticing and describing colors, shapes and textures through games of "I spy."

★ Use riddles that describe the answer to something. For example: "Guess who is coming to visit? She has grey hair, wears glasses, calls you Sweetie Pie, makes cookies, loves you very much...."

★ After doing something fun, like playing out in the snow, ask your child what the experience was like. Keep asking questions to get into the colorful details.

★ Each season, go on a visual adventure. Observe how colors and textures are changing. Look for signs of the seasons changing.

★ Compile a bin of art materials for your child to create with as she wishes.

Draw an imaginary pet that your family might like to own...or might not!

Skill #9: Enjoy and Use Fantasy

> like nonsense, it wakes up the brain cells. Fantasy is a necessary ingredient in living, it's a way of looking at life through the wrong end of a telescope. Which is what I do, and that enables you to laugh at life's realities. — Dr. Seuss

What is Enjoy and Use Fantasy?

Enjoy and Use Fantasy is about using the imagination, pretending, dreaming, acting, role-playing, improvising, telling stories, freely playing with possibilities, and asking "What if...?" The enjoyment of imagination usually comes more easily for children. It can often be difficult for adults to enjoy fantasy. If you are one of these adults, try giving your imagination permission to explore, and enjoy the ride.

Why is it important for creativity?

When we are able to *Enjoy and Use Fantasy,* we can let our imaginations take over and lead us to new possibilities. Imagining possibilities is very important for creative thinking, because without it, we can get boxed into a limiting paradigm, seeing things from only a concrete and singular perspective. Imagining possibilities expands our perspective from what we know and personally experience to what else is and what could be. It helps us explore and experiment with our emotions, thoughts, and ideas, and see where and how those things connect. Using fantasy helps children get to know and cope with their emotions, figure things out, and explore cause and effect relationships. As children grow, this skill will help them to share and understand ideas and emotions with others, use past and present experiences to problem-solve for the future, play and relate to others in meaningful ways, learn and apply knowledge, and engage more deeply in their life experiences.

A Story

One Saturday morning, my kids and I (Cyndi) pulled up to our local playground, which was populated with children. As my son came out of the car, a little boy with wild hair whom we did not know came running up to him.

"We have to find the treasure!" he shouted with enthusiasm.

My son did not hesitate. "Where do you think it could be?" he replied with equal zeal.

"This way! You have to come with me! This way!"

And on went my two children with a whole group of kids chasing after the imaginary treasure.

I was in a complete state of awe as I watched the story unfold. One child took over as leader and declared himself a head pirate, and he led the other pirates on a path across the desert (the playground), up and down the steps of the imaginary ship, across the wildfire (the monkey bars), and down the slippery mud slope (the slide) to where the actual treasure (which happened to be a pile of wood chips) was located. When the group of children found the treasure, they all celebrated with high fives and shouts of "Hooray!"

The children did not plan. They did not argue. They simply went with each other on the journey of their imaginations.

Using fantasy helps children to get to know and cope with their emotions, figure things out, and explore cause and effect relationships.

Cultivate the Language of Enjoy and Use Fantasy

Use words and phrases such as:

★ Imagine if...

★ Imagine that...

★ What if...

★ Can you imagine...?

★ Once upon a time...

★ Let's pretend...

★ You have a great imagination!

★ It's fun to play with you!

★ Let's use our imaginations.

★ Tell me a story.

Set the Tone!

★ Allow yourself to travel into your child's fantasy world. Follow your child's lead and enjoy the journey.

★ Have fun!

★ Embrace the actor in you. You might discover that you make a great knight in shining armor, lion tamer, or firefighter.

★ Do your best to be mindful in the moment and fully immerse yourself in the scenario.

★ Give yourself permission to be silly.

★ Be curious.

★ Look for opportunities to tell stories to your child.

★ Set aside time for using and enjoying fantasy with your child.

Give It a Go!

★ Have a discussion with your child about imagination. What is it? When do we use it? Talk about the differences between real and pretend. This is especially helpful with emotions about fear. Talk about how it is fun to pretend to be monsters, but remember there are no real monsters.

★ Go through your closet and create a bin of old clothes to be used for dress up. That ugly old bridesmaid dress can instantly transform into a princess dress! An old apron or pillowcase can transform into a magical cape.

★ Pretend to be a doctor, a teacher, the mailman, grandma, etc.

★ Create a "magic wand." Make some magical things happen. Transform your child into an animal, use it to take turns and talk or tell stories. Make wishes.

★ Act out a favorite story, poem, or song. Become the characters, make up different voices.

★ Bring out old Halloween costumes and use them in play.

★ Read the classic fairy tales, fables, and Mother Goose rhymes, as well as the parodies of those tales and rhymes.

★ Make a costume together. Draw the design out together, and go to the store to buy materials together. Work on creating the costume.

★ Write and illustrate a book together.

★ Introduce your child to a variety of creation stories. There are some vivid and beautiful stories about how the world came into existence.

★ Make a stage and put on a play, skit, dance, rock show, etc.

★ Make a TV with a cardboard box, get inside, and act out shows for each other, make a family news channel, etc.

★ Create a theme night based on your child's interests. Live by the theme for the night. A possible theme is cats: dress up as cats, eat things that cats might eat for dinner, watch a cat video, etc.

★ Have dinner time as kings and queens. Use your fancy dishes, make crowns, dress up, and pretend to be kings and queens at a royal banquet.

★ Tell your child vivid stories about your own childhood.

★ Create imaginary animals (pink cats, flying dogs, singing elephants).

Make up a title for a book you and your child could write together. Design the cover and draw it here.

★ Wrap up a box with an ordinary object inside and when you open it, pretend it has magical properties (a magic spool of thread, spoon, rock...). Act out the magic. Tell stories about what you find in the box.

★ Play the "what if" game: What if you were a lion? Yes, let's be lions (enact the lion). What if we were basketball players? Yes, let's be basketball players (enact the basketball players).

★ Cut out pictures from a magazine and create a story with the images.

★ Draw a scribble and then tell a story about how the scribble came to be.

★ Play family charades with simple words (giraffe, race car, hot, dancing, etc.).

★ Superhero fun: Imagine that you and your child are superheroes. Make costumes together: capes, masks, emblems, etc. Create a hideout. Explore your superpowers. Choose a name. Help people! Save the day!

★ Play "Imagine That!" Write characters, actions, etc., on small pieces of paper and put them in a box. Pull a piece of paper from the box and imagine that you are that character or doing that action. Have fun. Keep adding possibilities to the box with your child.

★   Bath time adventures: mermaids, fish, sharks, pirates, scuba divers—the possibilities are great and endless. Use your imagination and some small toys, props, wash cloths, etc., and transform your bath into a different world.

★   Make a grocery store trip an adventure/mission to find the items on your list. Give your child clues to find the item on the shelf. Be pirates looking for treasure, knights on a quest, or explorers on uncharted land.

★   Pretend to be spelunkers. Explore the caves of the bed sheets, under tables, closets, and the attic.

★   Lay out a small rug and go on a flying carpet adventure!

★   Go to see a professional storyteller. Visit a local storytelling group.

★   Learn the art of storytelling. Tell the stories of your family/ancestors.

★   Host a storytelling night. Invite each guest to read or tell a story.

★   Buy several different hats, and use them as magical hats. Perhaps each hat has different magical properties....

Create a new superhero (or superhero duo or trio).
What is your superhero name?
What outfit does your superhero wear?
What superpowers do you have?

★ Visit the zoo, then create your own zoo where you can be different animals.

★ Invite an imaginary person over for dinner and pretend to have a conversation with him/her.

★ Find some short and simple guided visualizations for children, or create your own. Invite your child to relax and close his eyes and imagine the things you are saying.

Keep It Going!

★ Ask interesting questions that spark the imagination. What would it be like to be a family of bunnies? What would happen if our feet were roller skates? Where do you think the bees go in wintertime?

★ Use role-playing as a tool for social, emotional, and behavioral development. Try using it when you are teaching your child about appropriate behavior in specific circumstances, or for a situation that causes your child anxiety, or acting out and reframing a distressing incident.

★ Talk about night dreaming with your child. Tell your child about your dreams and ask about his dreams.

★ Use role-playing as a learning tool. Try acting out together something that your child is learning such as how plants grow. Take on the roles of seeds, rain, and sun, and act out the process. Keep using this technique as your child grows and encounters more complex concepts.

★ When your child is having a bad day, have her imagine something that makes her happy. Help your child to imagine a happy and peaceful place that she can go to when she is distressed.

★ Incorporate fantasy into birthday parties. Think of ways that pretend play can be incorporated into the event. Bring props for children to use, make up a game that uses imagination, invite guests to dress up, etc.

★ Keep reading to your child as he grows. Read stories, fables, fairy tales, myths, etc. Keep fantasy a part of your child's life.

★ When solving problems as a family, use imagination and fantasy to think of unique ideas. Some great ideas can come from this, and it can also bring a lighter mood to a difficult situation.

With your child, draw as many emotions as you can think of, and label them.

Skill #10: Be Aware of Emotions

Feelings are much like waves, we can't stop them from coming but we can choose which one to surf. – Jonatan Mårtensson

What is Be Aware of Emotions?

Be Aware of Emotions refers to the awareness and management of emotional states. It is about the recognition of and response to our own emotions, as well the emotional states of others. In essence, this skill is about emotional intelligence.

Our ability to *Be Aware of Emotions* develops as we grow. Young children have different capacities to recognize and use emotions than babies, teenagers or adults. As parents, we can help our children develop emotional awareness and empathy, which can lead to rich, healthy and positive emotional landscapes that will benefit them throughout their lives.

Why is it important for creativity?

Emotions are powerful fuel for our thoughts and actions. At our best, our emotions can give us energy, meaning and purpose, and help us succeed and flourish. At our worst, they can throw us into crisis, limit our capabilities, and hinder us from growth and new experiences. Our emotional states can impact our mindsets, our thinking, and our ability to creatively solve problems.

Positive emotions benefit creativity. Joy, hope, pride, interest, love, inspiration, awe, and amusement are all examples of positive emotions that benefit creative thinking and problem solving. Negative emotions such as fear, anxiety, despair, and shame, when not acknowledged and addressed, can block creativity and life satisfaction. *Being Aware of Emotions* can help to cultivate positivity, and to work through negativity, allowing us to harness our creative potentials.

A Story

I (Cyndi) am always amazed at how two kids who come from the same two parents can be so completely different. And while I believe that most kids have a high level of curiosity, playfulness, and mindfulness, I also believe that kids have varying levels of emotional awareness and intensity.

One day, as I was walking across the kitchen, I slid on a toy car and did the accidental fall dance (I can laugh about it now), landing very hard on my back. As I lay on the floor in tears, my two-year-old daughter ran over to me. "Are you okay Mommy?" she asked gently.

She grabbed my cheeks, gave me a kiss and said, "It's okay Mommy. You be okay."

I glanced over at my three-year-old son, who had run over to play with his toy trains when I fell, completely oblivious to my pain.

I have spent a considerable amount of time trying to teach my son to be aware of other people's emotions. When a friend falls at playgroup, we practice going over, checking with the friend to make sure he is okay, and acknowledging the fact that he might be sad. At this point, I realized that my son could use a bit more practice in that area.

On the flip side, my son has never been one for emotional meltdowns or tantrums. If he asks for a treat at the store and I tell him no because we will be eating dinner shortly, he generally understands. He might whine, but he doesn't have a fit. My empathetic daughter, on the other hand, will go into a full-blown meltdown at even the smallest "no." She will throw herself on the floor, roll around, stomp off, and, if at home, go strum the guitar in our dining room. With her, I spend a great deal of time helping her to manage her emotions.

Two very different reactions, and two very different children.

For this section, we would like you to think about your own children and their awareness of emotions—both their own and those of others.

Cultivate the Language of Be Aware of Emotions

Use words to name feelings: frustrated, angry, happy, joyful, sad, sorry, proud, startled, etc. Also, use words and phrases such as:

★   You look/sound _____ (frustrated, excited, mad, etc.).

★   How do you feel about that?

★   What does that emotion feel like in your body?

★   I notice _____ (your fists are clenched, you are looking at the floor, etc.). Are you feeling _____ (angry, sad, etc.)?

★   I am feeling....

★   How do you think he/she is feeling?

★   I see you are _____. What happened?

★   I noticed that _____. How do you feel about that?

Set the Tone!

★   Be observant of your child's emotions and acknowledge them. When you see your child run into a corner when a stranger comes into the room, acknowledge it. "I can see that you are feeling shy about Mr. Johnson coming over." "You look frustrated. Are you feeling frustrated?"

★   Watch for and point out emotions of others—with friends, on television, and in books. When a friend falls down, take the time to explain: "Chase is very sad because he fell down and scraped his leg."

★   Be aware of and acknowledge your own emotions and point them out to your child. "Mommy is feeling happy because it is a beautiful sunny day!" "I am feeling frustrated because this is a hard task."

★   Help your child to describe her emotions in words, images, or movements.

★   Turn fears into something silly. For example: If your child is afraid of the vacuum cleaner, dress it up, draw a funny picture of it, give it a silly name, battle it with super powers, etc.

★   Help your child to differentiate between real scary and pretend scary, and between being scared and being startled.

★ Be aware of your child's temperament. Some kids have intense emotions, some are more laid back, and some are very sensitive. Get to know the emotional landscape of your child and help your child navigate it.

★ Smile at people.

★ Show your child how you connect with other people: smiling, talking, shaking hands, making eye contact, asking questions, sending cards, attending parties, being polite, listening, taking turns, sharing, etc.

★ Show your child how you express your empathy.

★ Avoid trying to change your child's emotional state before you understand it. For example, resist telling your child to stop crying. Rather, first discover the reason behind the emotion. This will help you connect with your child and help your child to understand the emotions of the situation.

★ When your child is distressed, it can often help to match his tone, expression, and body language and then slowly help him calm down.

★ Work to understand your own emotions and how you express them.

★ Be honest about your emotions. You do not need to go into details, but if your child asks if you are sad, tell him the truth. This can help him see emotions as a normal and good part of life, and he will witness different ways to manage and express emotions.

★ Remember that kids develop emotionally in different ways. Do not worry if your child seems to be developing emotional skills more slowly.

Give It a Go!

★ Take photographs of things that make your child happy (or have your child take the pictures). Turn the pictures into a collage for his bedroom.

★ Create a joy journal. Each night, ask your child what made him happy that day, and write it in his journal, or have him draw a picture of it in the journal. Or, at the dinner table, simply talk about the happy things that occurred during the day.

★ Download and print an emotions chart that shows a variety of emotions. Post the chart on a wall so your child can see it and make use of it when appropriate.

★ Pick out stories that clearly show characters with emotions. ("Jack and the Beanstalk" is a great example. As you read the story to your child, point out Jack's feelings throughout the story.)

★   Ask your child to draw you a picture of how she is feeling.

★   Ask your child to portray with her body how she feels when she is sad, angry, happy, etc.

★   Borrow books from the library that talk about your child's emotions. We like The Way I Feel, by Janas Cain and Today I feel Silly, by Jamie Lee Curtis. As you read about each emotion, show your child what the face looks like, and explain how the body feels.

★   Listen to different kinds of music and ask your child how the music makes him feel. Explore the feelings evoked by the music through movement or drawing.

★   While sitting in a restaurant or shopping place, be aware of emotions of other people, and point them out. "That little boy looks happy because he is eating ice cream!" "That baby is crying. Do you think the baby is upset? Why do you think the baby could be upset?"

★   Think about the colors of emotion: What color could represent happy? What color could represent sad?

★   Play Emotion Charades: Write down different emotions and put them in a hat or box. Pull an emotion out and act it out.

★ Tell each other stories that include different emotions.

★ Include emotions when you are playing pretend with your child. For example, if you are pretending to be knights fighting a fierce dragon, pretend to be scared, then find your courage.

★ Create a line drawing: Draw happy, sad, scared, startled, etc. emotions with one line.

★ Engage in a feelings dance: Can you make up a dance that shows me how you are feeling?

★ Find colorful objects around the house, such as Goldfish Colors crackers, jelly beans, colored blocks, or beads. Each color represents a feeling (gold = proud, green = jealous, red = angry, etc.). You and your child each take turns picking an object from the bag and sharing a story about a time you felt the emotion represented by the color chosen.

★ Happiness Hunt: Let your child use a camera, and have him take pictures of things that make him happy. Put the photos on the wall or make a collage. Make copies and send them as greeting cards to extended family or friends.

★ Pick a feeling and work with your child to make a collage that illustrates that feeling. Use pictures from magazines, family photos, drawings, or words to illustrate what that feeling is like for your child.

★ Act out emotions with your child. Pretend to be happy, sad, frustrated, excited, angry, cranky, etc. Use your face, body, and voice to express your emotions. Choose an emotion and act it out, or take turns guessing the emotion being expressed. Try these in front of a mirror.

★ Pick a positive emotion and design an entire day around that emotion: Love Day, Happy Day, Thankful Day, etc. Make food, dress up, read books, play games—do things that relate to that emotion.

★ Have a Happy Party. Make invitations and have your child choose food, games, music, etc., that make her happy.

★ Make masks of different emotions. Use them to play.

★ Make up feeling songs or modify other songs, like "If you're happy and you know it."

★ Make up a Happy Dance, and do it together when someone is happy.

★ Make up a "shake off the frustration" movement.

★ Use sidewalk chalk and write positive messages or draw pictures throughout your neighborhood. Talk about how people will see the messages and feel happy.

★ Make a family "Joy List" of things that bring joy to each of your family members.

★ Draw a "thank you" picture for a family member or friend that shows something that you and your child appreciate about that person. Give or mail it to them as a special surprise.

★ Have your child make thank you cards and use them when a thank you note could be sent.

★ Tell stories about the childhood memories you have that deal with emotions. Describe a time when you felt sad or angry or excited.

> Use sidewalk chalk and write positive messages or draw pictures throughout your neighborhood.

Kep It Going!

★ Make connections between the emotions of your child and stories you have read with your child, or TV shows and movies you have seen together.

★ Talk to your child about courage. Show how courage is part of fear, facing it, and moving through it. Talk about the things that make you afraid, and how you face those fears. Talk about people who are courageous: firefighters, superheroes, people you and your child know, knights, astronauts, etc.

★ Create a "calm down spot" or peaceful place in your house, a special place where any family member can go to cool down, relax, and refresh. Make it comfortable and add objects or quiet meditative activities that can be used to relax.

★ Check in with your child daily to see how he is feeling and discuss why he is feeling the way he is.

★ At dinner or sometime during the day, ask each family member to think of something that he/she is grateful for. Share and discuss.

★ Try journaling with your child. Write about one good experience that happened during the day. Write a new gratitude each day.

★ Start a gratitude journal or place to document the little and big things you and your child are grateful for. Make a family gratitude poster: "We are grateful for...." Add things every day, keep the poster up and read it together every so often.

★ When celebrating holidays, include the emotions that are associated with it.

★ Get daily exercise as a family.

★ As a family, engage in acts of kindness in your home, community and social networks.

★ Look for new ways to cultivate positive emotions as a family.

★ Build and sustain close relationships in your family. This leads to support needed when times get tough.

How do you feel after reading to this point in the book? What are the first three things you will do?

3

Afterword: Extend the Learning

What questions do you have for the authors?
Write them here, then tweet them to @ICSCreativity,
with the hastag #SandwichSpaceship.

The End of This Journey: Authors' Reflections on Getting Here

As we come to the end of this book with you, the reader, we are reflecting on the journey we took as authors in creating it. Our sons were toddlers when we first began our collaboration. Now, five years later, our boys are in the second and third grade!

Now that our children are in school, we recognize—even more—the importance of developing creative thinking skills at an early age. Once your children go into school, things change. The focus on play and discovery shifts to finding the "right" answers and learning the "appropriate" ways to do things. Although it comes out as an either-or, we consider it to be more of a yes-and.

Yes: there are some things that have right answers; there are appropriate and accepted ways to do things. And: we need to help our children preserve their natural creative abilities—to be curious, open-minded, playful, and engaged in learning. We need to continue to help them develop their abilities to embrace challenges and opportunities as they face more complex problems in school and in life. Utilizing the creative thinking skills found in this book will allow our children to not only navigate these obstacles, but to accept the inevitable and endless change that comes with growing up.

This book has been such a joy to write, as it has come from our personal experiences, our work as creativity practitioners, and what we are most passionate about: raising creative, independent, and resilient kids.

The journey of writing this book over the past five years was filled with changes, challenges, and opportunities for us and our families. Cyndi had another child, moved twice, and finished her doctoral degree. Michaelene moved, made career changes, got married, helped her son transition into school, and experienced the loss of her mother. These challenges and changes happen for all families in one form or another. In our families, we used creative thinking skills and approached these challenges with a creative mindset. Creativity is more than a set of skills. It can be a philosophy, a mindset, and an empowering way of approaching and living life fully.

The Journey Continues for All of Us

The book has been written, but of course we are still parents, just like you are. And for all of us, that journey continues. So, what now?

If you haven't already, the first thing to do is try some of this out. This book is just chock-full of ideas for developing creativity skills in every member of your family.

Beyond that, this book is much more than a set of skills and fun activities. Your kids will certainly outgrow many/most/all of the activities here, so remember that the activities are a vehicle for developing the skills; in the end, it is the skills that matter. It is our hope that this book is merely the first part of the lifelong journey you take with your family in embracing creativity as a powerful mindset and way of living.

Our sincerest wish for you and your family is that creativity becomes a part of your daily lives.

We believe that when people embrace their creativity they empower their lives, and when people are empowered they can transform not only their lives, but also the lives of those around them: neighbors and neighborhoods, schoolmates and schools, community members and entire communities. And why not the world? The creative mind touches so many, and good ideas and behaviors are contagious.

Affirmations

There is just one more thing we want to share with you: on the next page is a set of affirmations for living a creative life as a family. These affirmations are based on the skills in this book. You can use these affirmations just as they are (there's a printable version at icscpress.com), or stretch your creativity wings and create your own family affirmations.

Thank you for sharing this journey with us. We wish you and your family a creative, meaningful and joyful life together!

Affirmations

Curiosity: We are curious and take time for discovery.

Mindfulness: We practice mindfulness and focus on the present moment.

Embrace Challenges: We build our resiliency and look for the wisdom and opportunity in challenges.

Look at it another way: We look at things in new ways and seek different perspectives.

Produce and Consider Many Alternatives: We look for and generate more than one option.

Playfulness: We take time to play.

Make it Swing! Make it Ring!: We sing, dance, and move our way through life.

Visualize it Richly and Colorfully: We are inspired by the vividness of the world.

Enjoy and Use Fantasy: We engage with imaginary worlds.

Be Aware of Emotions: We fuel our emotions in positive ways.

Acknowledgments

Cyndi Burnett

To my amazing writing partner, friend, colleague, and fellow mom, Michaelene Dawson-Globus. WE DID IT! This has been an incredible journey with you and I am so grateful to have you in my life.

To my lightbulb, funny, supportive husband, Andy Burnett. Every day I am grateful for finding a partner who shares a vision for creativity and education in every facet of our lives, especially our home! Thanks for being my rock.

To my son, James, who has taught me more about creative thinking than any other academic journal on the topic. Thank you for helping me to search for the positives, for looking at things from different perspectives, and for your wondrous enthusiasm for life.

To my daughter, Emily, whose passion and motivation inspires my creativity every day. Thank you for asking so many questions, for dancing to any sound resembling a beat, and for tackling challenges with all of your heart.

Thank you to the fabulous Paul Reali, of ICSC Press, for editing and working with this document. To my incredible professional assistant, Julia Figliotti, thank you for reading this book over and over and over again.

To my parents and brothers and sisters—thank you for creating a home life where passion, motivation, and working hard were the norm.

Finally, to my team at the International Center for Studies in Creativity, thanks for making me laugh, think, problem solve, and eat cake every single day I walk into the office.

Michaelene Dawson-Globus

To my Mom, Mary Ann Dawson, who has passed to her next great adventure. Thank you for instilling in me the foundation of creativity and being a woman of light, love and compassion. You live on in my spirit and my work. I wish you were here.

To Sam, who is the catalyst. You are the most interesting person I have ever met. You inspire me every day to grow, learn and create. I love you with a love that is as big as the expanding universe!

To my husband Chris, whose support, love and partnership keeps it all going. Go Team!

To my siblings, John, Steve, and Amanda for always having my back and being awesome people to grow-up with in this crazy world.

To my Dad for giving our family a life that allowed creativity to flourish, for telling us stories and for being a good man.

To Anthony for all you do to make life beautiful.

To Ryan for being an important part of my family and Sam's first love.

To the ICSC community for igniting my passion for creativity.

To Paul for editing this book and believing in its message.

To the fabulous Cyndi Burnett, my writing partner, teacher, colleague and friend. It has been a joy to create this book, and grow as a mother with you.

About the Authors

Dr. Cyndi Burnett is an Assistant Professor at the International Center for Studies in Creativity at SUNY Buffalo State. She has a Bachelor of Fine Arts in Theater, a Master of Science in Creativity, and a Doctorate of Education in Curriculum, Teaching and Learning, all of which she uses to help "ignite creativity around the world." Specifically, she focuses her work on the use of creative models and techniques with children. Cyndi is passionate about working with educators to bring creative thinking into the classroom, and working with her family to bring creative thinking into their home. When she's not teaching or writing, Cyndi enjoys cooking, singing show tunes, and having dance parties with her 5- and 7-year old kids, James and Emily. Cyndi was featured in an article in the *New York Times* titled, "Creativity Becomes an Academic Discipline." She is the co-editor of the *Big Questions in Creativity* book series, and co-author of the book *Weaving Creativity into Every Strand of Your Curriculum.*

Michaelene Dawson-Globus is an Adjunct Instructor at the International Center for Studies in Creativity at SUNY Buffalo State. She has a Master of Science in Creativity. Michaelene leads workshops, training classes, and facilitations on a variety of topics including: creative teaching and learning, creative problem solving, change leadership, diversity, and social empowerment. Michaelene is also a social justice facilitator for The National Federation for Just Communities of Western New York. Michaelene lives in Western NY with her husband Chris and her 8-year old Adventure Buddy, Sam.

The International Center for Studies in Creativity

Creativity, creative problem solving, and change leadership play a major role in today's workplace. Professional success is linked to the ability to master creativity, to operate as a creative problem solver, to innovate and to lead change. The need for people to cope with and direct change in their lives and in their organizations has become increasingly apparent. At the International Center for Studies in Creativity (ICSC), we strive to develop and nurture critical life skills in our students. The approaches we teach are applied successfully to educational, business, and industrial settings. Our graduates report that the skills and lessons learned at the ICSC have had a profound impact on their lives and organizations.

The ICSC is recognized for offering "The Credential in Creativity" for more than 40 years, a Master of Science degree and a graduate certificate in Creativity and Change Leadership. These programs are designed to provide professionals with the necessary skills to become transformational leaders in their organizations and communities. With our international reputation, we attract students from around the world. The Master of Science and graduate certificate are available on campus, as well as to distance learners.

The ICSC is a unique academic unit within SUNY Buffalo State. Since 1967, we have trained students, groups, teams and organizations to become more effective creative thinkers and problem solvers and to instill these skills in others. As the first school to offer a Master of Science degree in creativity, the ICSC has achieved an international reputation for scholarly research and teaching that focuses on developing creativity, leadership, decision-making and problem-solving skills. We invite you to explore the many opportunities that are available through our educational programs. Please visit creativity.buffalostate.edu.

ICSC Press

Created in 2012, ICSC Press is the imprint of the International Center for Studies in Creativity. The mission of the press supports the vision of the Center to ignite creativity around the world, facilitating the recognition of creative thinking as an essential life skill.

ICSC Press's goal is to put the work of our best teachers, thinkers, and practitioners into the hands of a wide audience, making titles available quickly and in multiple formats, both paper and electronic.

To learn more, to purchase titles, or to submit a proposal, visit icscpress.com.

CPSIA information can be obtained
at www.ICGtesting.com
Printed in the USA
LVOW05s0425090116

469712LV00009B/37/P